THE
NATIONAL PARKS

DISCOVER ALL 62 PARKS
OF THE UNITED STATES

Written by
Stefanie Payne

DK | Penguin Random House

Senior editors Carrie Love, Jolyon Goddard,
Roohi Sehgal
Project editor Olivia Stanford
Editor Katie Lawrence
Assistant editors Becky Walsh, Niharika Prabhakar
Project art editors Jaileen Kaur, Roohi Rais, Kanika Kalra
Art editor Mohd Zishan
Assistant art editor Bhagyashree Nayak
Executive editor, Americanization Lori Cates Hand
Jacket coordinator Issy Walsh
Jacket designer Sonny Flynn
DTP designers Sachin Gupta, Dheeraj Singh,
Nand Kishor Acharya
Picture researchers Sakshi Saluja, Rituraj Singh
Production editor Siu Yin Chan
Production controller Basia Ossowska
Managing editor Monica Saigal
Managing art editor Ivy Sengupta
Delhi team head Malavika Talukder
Senior commissioning designer Fiona Macdonald
Publishing manager Francesca Young
Creative director Helen Senior
Publishing director Sarah Larter

Illustrators Abby Cook,
Erin Brown c/o Collaborate Agency
Subject consultants Dr Kim Bryan,
Mike Gerrard, Eric Peterson

First American Edition, 2020
Published in the United States by DK Publishing
1745 Broadway, 20th Floor, New York, NY 10019

Copyright © 2020 Dorling Kindersley Limited
DK, a Division of Penguin Random House LLC
23 24 25 10 9 8 7 6
007–320926–Oct/2020

A catalog record for this book is
available from the Library of Congress.
ISBN 978-0-7440-2429-6

DK books are available at special discounts when purchased in bulk
for sales promotions, premiums, fund-raising, or educational use.
For details, contact: DK Publishing Special Markets,
1745 Broadway, 20th Floor, New York, NY 10019
SpecialSales@dk.com

Printed and bound in China

www.dk.com

MIX
Paper | Supporting
responsible forestry
FSC™ C018179

This book was made with Forest
Stewardship Council™ certified
paper—one small step in DK's
commitment to a sustainable future.
For more information go to
www.dk.com/our-green-pledge

CONTENTS

WHAT IS A NATIONAL PARK?

National parks are areas of outstanding beauty. They are established by acts of Congress and given the highest level of protection by the Department of the Interior. Managed by the National Park Service, the parks' vast landscapes, wildernesses, forests, waterways, caves, cultural heritage, and wildlife are safeguarded for the enjoyment of us all.

American kestrel

Established in 2019, **White Sands** in New Mexico is the **newest** national park.

Harbor seals lounge on icebergs in Glacier Bay National Park and Preserve.

WHAT IS A PRESERVE?

Several national parks, especially those in Alaska, are coupled with a national preserve. These areas often allow hunting, trapping, and fishing, so that longstanding communities can carry on a traditional way of life. Oil and gas exploration and mining are also allowed in some preserves.

National parks attract hikers from all over the world.

Look for this stamp in the book to see the parks with preserves.

NATIONAL PARK & PRESERVE

4

CARING FOR THE PARKS

Starting in 1933 with the Civilian Conservation Corps and continuing today with rangers and volunteers, dedicated workers are responsible for maintaining the parks. They construct new trails, roads, and buildings, fight fires, control floods, perform clean-ups, help in rescue operations, and start conservation projects.

Volunteers at Saguaro National Park remove invasive buffel grass to protect native plants.

THE FACTS

How many are there?: 62 national parks; seven are also preserves

When was the National Park Service founded?: 1916

Visitors each year: More than 84 million

First park: Yellowstone; established in 1872

Most visited park: Great Smoky Mountains

Least visited park: Gates of the Arctic

Park rangers can provide information about the best places to see in a park.

Florida manatee

JOBS IN THE PARKS

National Park Service rangers provide many important services in the parks, including teaching classes and restoring habitats. Park police protect visitors and the parks' natural resources. Managers and operational staff ensure the best experience for all visitors.

NATIONAL PARKS OF THE UNITED STATES

The United States has 62 national parks, protecting a wide range of different habitats. There are parks across the country and also in the US Virgin Islands and American Samoa.

Alaska inset:
ARCTIC OCEAN
Kobuk Valley
Gates of the Arctic
ALASKA
Wrangell-St. Elias
Denali
Lake Clark
Glacier Bay
Katmai
Kenai Fjords
Gulf of Alaska

Hawai'i inset:
PACIFIC OCEAN
Haleakalā
HAWAI'I
Hawai'i Volcanoes

American Samoa inset:
National Park of American Samoa
AMERICAN SAMOA
PACIFIC OCEAN

Main map:
Olympic
North Cascades
WASHINGTON
Glacier
Mount Rainier
OREGON
IDAHO
MONTANA
NORTH DAKOTA
Theodore Roosevelt
SOUTH DAKOTA
Crater Lake
Yellowstone
Grand Teton
Redwood
Badlands
Wind Cave
PACIFIC OCEAN
Lassen Volcanic
CALIFORNIA
NEVADA
WYOMING
NEBRASKA
UTAH
COLORADO
Rocky Mountain
Yosemite
Great Basin
Capitol Reef
Arches
Black Canyon of the Gunnison
Pinnacles
Death Valley
Zion
Canyonlands
Great Sand Dunes
Sequoia and Kings Canyon
Bryce Canyon
Mesa Verde
Grand Canyon
ARIZONA
Channel Islands
Joshua Tree
Petrified Forest
NEW MEXICO
TEXAS
Saguaro
White Sands
Carlsbad Caverns
Guadalupe Mountains
Big Bend

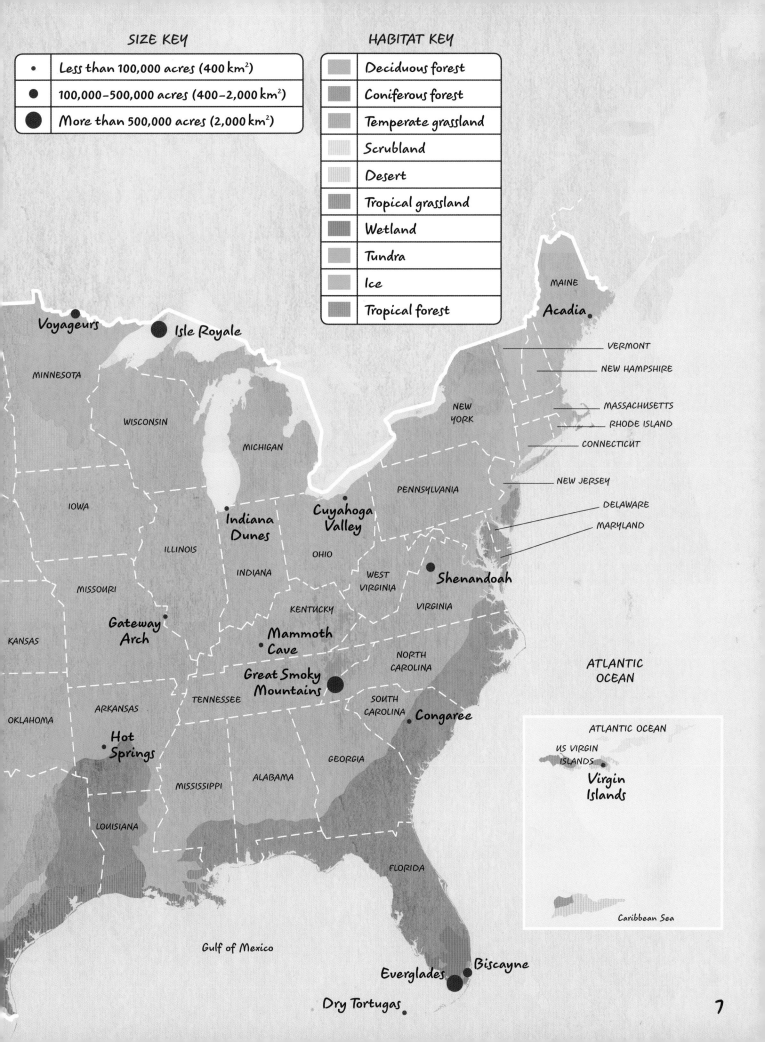

SIZE KEY

- • Less than 100,000 acres (400 km²)
- ● 100,000–500,000 acres (400–2,000 km²)
- ⬤ More than 500,000 acres (2,000 km²)

HABITAT KEY

- Deciduous forest
- Coniferous forest
- Temperate grassland
- Scrubland
- Desert
- Tropical grassland
- Wetland
- Tundra
- Ice
- Tropical forest

MAINE

Acadia

VERMONT

NEW HAMPSHIRE

MASSACHUSETTS

RHODE ISLAND

CONNECTICUT

NEW JERSEY

DELAWARE

MARYLAND

NEW YORK

PENNSYLVANIA

Voyageurs

Isle Royale

MINNESOTA

WISCONSIN

MICHIGAN

IOWA

Indiana Dunes

Cuyahoga Valley

ILLINOIS

INDIANA

OHIO

WEST VIRGINIA

Shenandoah

VIRGINIA

MISSOURI

Gateway Arch

KANSAS

KENTUCKY

Mammoth Cave

Great Smoky Mountains

TENNESSEE

NORTH CAROLINA

SOUTH CAROLINA

Congaree

ATLANTIC OCEAN

OKLAHOMA

ARKANSAS

Hot Springs

GEORGIA

ALABAMA

MISSISSIPPI

LOUISIANA

FLORIDA

Gulf of Mexico

ATLANTIC OCEAN

US VIRGIN ISLANDS

Virgin Islands

Caribbean Sea

Everglades

Biscayne

Dry Tortugas

WRANGELL– ST. ELIAS

NATIONAL PARK & PRESERVE

ALASKA ESTABLISHED 1980

Wrangell–St. Elias National Park and Preserve is home to sprawling glaciers, active volcanoes, jagged mountains, and a variety of plants and animals. It is the largest national park in the United States. The park was named for the Wrangell and the St. Elias mountain ranges, which both run through the park.

THE FACTS

Size: 13,175,791 acres (53,320.53 km²)
Highest point: 18,008 ft (5,489 m) at Mount St. Elias
Visitors each year: Almost 75,000

THE WRANGELL MOUNTAINS

These mountains were once volcanic, but only Mount Wrangell remains active. Wrangell is a shield volcano, which means that runny lava flowed out of it in layers to create a huge dome shape. Its copper-rich rocks were once mined.

Male Steller sea lions weigh up to 2,500 lb (1,134 kg).

STELLER SEA LION

Steller sea lions are the biggest sea lions. They propel themselves through water with their front flippers and steer with the back ones. The flippers can also be used for moving on land. Sea lions bark to communicate with each other.

8

The **willow ptarmigan's** feathered feet act like **snowshoes** to help it walk on snow.

HUBBARD GLACIER

Glaciers cover more than a third of Wrangell–St. Elias. Hubbard Glacier is 7 miles (11 km) wide and flows 76 miles (122 km) to the sea. The ice falling off its face is as much as 500 years old.

Meadows of fireweed can be seen in the park.

FUN IN THE SNOW

In the winter months, snowmobiles—called snow machines in Alaska—hikers, and skiers are regularly seen crossing the snowfields of the park.

PARK HABITATS

 Snow and ice

Mountain

Coniferous forest

River

Massive icefields in the mountain ranges feed rivers of ice in the park. In lower areas, animals live in the lakes, streams, coniferous forests, and grassy areas.

9

COASTAL MOUNTAINS

The Wrangell and St. Elias mountain ranges block warm air from the sea, making the land behind them very cold. These two ranges are part of a chain of ranges, called the Pacific Coast Ranges, stretching along the western coast of North America, from Mexico to Alaska.

GATES OF THE ARCTIC

NATIONAL PARK & PRESERVE

ALASKA ESTABLISHED 1980

With no roads and no set campgrounds or trails, Gates of the Arctic National Park and Preserve is a completely wild landscape. The park is the farthest north of all the national parks—it's a land of natural treasures and extreme beauty, filled with wildlife, rivers, and mountains.

THE FACTS

Size: 8,472,506 acres (34,287.01 km²)
Highest point: 8,276 ft (2,523 m) at Mount Igikpak
Visitors each year: About 10,500

ARRIGETCH PEAKS

Mountaineers from all over the world come to this cluster of rugged peaks to test out their wilderness skills. The peaks have long been sacred to the Nunamiut people of northwest Alaska, who still live in the area.

The park attracts some of the most adventurous hikers and backpackers.

WALKER LAKE

This 14-mile (26-km) stretch of water allows Alaska Natives, living within the park's boundaries, and visitors to enjoy wilderness camping, paddling, and fishing on its shores.

The musk ox's long hair keeps it warm in the cold Alaskan climate.

MUSK OXEN

Unique to the far north, musk oxen are recognizable by their long hair and distinctive horns. They can be spotted grazing on the grassy flats of northern Alaska.

PARK HABITATS

 Tundra

 Mountain

River

Coniferous forest

Gates of the Arctic is located almost entirely above the Arctic Circle. Its rugged mountains surround six Wild and Scenic Rivers that flow next to forests and tundra.

Moss campion is found growing on the rocks and in the meadows of the park.

DENALI

ALASKA ESTABLISHED 1917

Denali National Park and Preserve is one of Alaska's most visited and well-known national parks. With only one road and millions of acres of wilderness, the park and preserve are home to a wide variety of plants and animals. Towering high above the park is North America's tallest peak—Denali.

DOGSLEDS

Since 1922, Denali's sled dogs and park rangers have teamed up to protect the park, while carrying on the Alaskan tradition of mushing (dogsledding). Today, Denali is the only national park with a working kennel.

Rangers offer dogsledding demonstrations every day in summer.

SPECTACULAR NORTHERN LIGHTS

In fall, winter, and early spring, a colorful light display in the sky, called the Northern Lights, can be seen in Denali and many other places in and near the Arctic.

FACTS

Size: 6,075,029 acres (24,584.77 km²)
Highest point: 20,310 ft (6,190 m) at Denali's peak
Visitors each year: More than 600,000

Monkshood flowers depend on bumblebees to pollinate them so they can produce seeds.

The scientific name for the Northern Lights is "Aurora Borealis."

PARK HABITATS

Snow and ice

Coniferous forest

Tundra

Mountain

Denali is known for its rugged landscape, featuring snowy peaks, tundra, and forests. The mountains in the park, including its namesake, "Denali," are covered with glacier ice.

Wood frogs in Denali have **adapted** to **survive** during cold winters.

LAND OF ICE

Mountain peaks poke out of the thick glacier ice. Mountaineers come from all over the world to climb the challenging rockfaces.

Mountaineering

KATMAI

ALASKA ESTABLISHED 1980

Katmai National Park and Preserve includes the Valley of Ten Thousand Smokes—the site of the world's largest volcanic eruption in the 20th century. Katmai is home to about 2,200 brown bears that feed on the fish in the wild rivers.

THE FACTS

Size: 4,093,228 acres (16,564.71 km^2)
Highest point: 7,605 ft (2,318 m) at Mount Denison
Visitors each year: More than 80,000

Arctic terns

MAKING OF THE CRATER LAKE

When the Novarupta volcano last erupted in 1912, a crater lake formed in Mount Katmai volcano. Today, it holds snow, glacial ice, and vibrantly colored water. The lake is about 800 ft (244 m) deep—it looks like a giant cauldron.

BROOKS FALLS

This waterfall is packed with salmon swimming upstream in summer, and then spawning in early fall. During this time, Brooks Falls is the perfect place for bears to find their dinner!

Sockeye salmon battle the waterfall's strong current as they swim upstream.

Horned puffins can be seen perching on the rocky islands off the coast of the park.

PARK HABITATS

 River

Snow and ice

 Lake

Mountain

Katmai has hundreds of miles of rivers and many lakes, which are home to fish and other wildlife. Active, snow-covered volcanoes form a spine along the eastern region of the park.

Northern geraniums add a pop of violet to the park's meadows.

Bears prefer the fattiest parts of salmon—the skin, brain, and eggs.

FISHING BEARS

Not all bears catch their fish in the same way. Some sit and wait at the top or bottom of Brooks Falls for the salmon to swim to them, while others snorkel to look for the fish. A few even steal fish from other bears!

LAKE CLARK

ALASKA ESTABLISHED 1980

There are no roads to Lake Clark National Park and Preserve—the only way to get there is by boat or aircraft. This remote area is home to mountain ranges, two active volcanoes, lakes, dense forests, and salmon-filled rivers. The park even contains temperate rainforests—where rainfall is high, but the temperature is mild.

About 50 pairs of **bald eagles** are known to nest in the park.

NATIONAL PARK ★ & PRESERVE

LAKE CLARK

Lake Clark is 42 miles (68 km) long and 5 miles (8 km) wide. It has a vibrant blue color from particles of rock that have washed into the water from the surrounding mountains. The Dena'ina Athabascan people named the lake Qizjeh Vena, meaning "place where people gather."

THE FACTS

Size: 4,030,110 acres (16,309.28 km²)
Highest point: 10,197 ft (3,108 m) at Redoubt Volcano
Visitors each year: More than 17,000

PARK HABITATS

 Lake

 Mountain

Coniferous forest

River

Lake Clark is surrounded by snow-covered mountains. Cascading from them are rivers and streams that flow into lakes, forests, and also tundra. The lake itself attracts many animals, inlcuding migrating salmon.

Inside the cabin is a wood-burning stove, fireplace, bed, and writing table.

PROENNEKE'S CABIN

Richard Louis Proenneke (1916–2003) was an American naturalist. He built a log cabin in the park near Upper Twin Lake, where he lived alone without running water or electricity for 30 years.

Each year an average of 372,000 sockeye, or red salmon, swim up the Newhalen River and enter the waters of Lake Clark National Park and Preserve.

Common cottongrass has fluffy, white seedheads.

REDOUBT VOLCANO

Mount Redoubt is a stratovolcano, which has a tall, conical shape. It is active and last erupted in 2009.

EUREKA SAND DUNES

The highest in California, these dunes rise to nearly 700 ft (213 m) in Eureka Valley. Winds sometimes cause sand falls (mini sand avalanches). As the sand moves, it makes a soft humming sound, earning it the nickname "singing sand."

Greater roadrunners can run as fast as 20 mph (32 kph).

GREATER ROADRUNNER

While Death Valley is a gathering point for many migrating birds, roadrunners live in the park all year. They are very quick, allowing them to easily catch insects, snakes, and lizards.

DEATH VALLEY

CALIFORNIA–NEVADA ESTABLISHED 1994

Death Valley National Park has many extremes. Long periods of drought are broken by brief rains that create vast fields of wildflowers. In summer the heat is scorching, and in winter the peaks are capped with snow. It holds the record as the hottest, driest, and lowest national park in the United States.

FACTS

Size: 3,408,407 acres (13,793.33 km^2)
Highest point: 11,049 ft (3,368 m) at Telescope Peak
Visitors each year: About 1.75 million

The bright flowers of the Mojave mound cactus bloom from April to June.

PARK HABITATS

🌵 **Desert**

⛰️ **Mountain**

🌾 **Wetland**

Death Valley stretches across a hot desert landscape. Sand dunes, rugged canyons, and salt flats extend beneath two mountain ranges that encircle the park. Despite the dryness, springs give plant and animal life a chance to survive in the hot climate.

The desert iguana is usually seen in sandy areas of the park.

Desert sunflower

A rare **explosion** of wildflowers in spring is known as a **super bloom**.

BADWATER BASIN

The lowest point in North America, this vast, flat field of salt causes a white shimmer on the horizon. When rainwater in the basin dries up in intense heat, the salt cracks into geometric shapes.

GLACIER BAY

National Park & Preserve

ALASKA ESTABLISHED 1980

There are more than 1,000 glistening glaciers in this national park and preserve. Glaciers are huge, slow-moving masses of ice and rock. Some of the park's glaciers flow all the way to the icy-cold sea, which supports a diversity of species, including seaweeds; crustaceans; fish; and marine mammals, such as whales.

PARK HABITATS

- Snow and ice
- Ocean
- Mountain
- Coniferous forest

Water and ice flow from high in the steep sculpted mountains, through forests and other habitats before reaching the ocean, which is rich in wildlife.

Kayaking around the park is a great way to explore Glacier Bay.

MARGERIE GLACIER

Rising more than 250 ft (76 m) above the bay, Margerie Glacier is an impressive sight. Sometimes large chunks of ice break away into the water with a loud booming sound. This breakage is called "glacier calving."

LIFE AMONG THE ICE

The waters of Glacier Bay are home to minke and humpback whales, and orcas, as well as harbor porpoises, seals, Steller sea lions, and sea otters.

Humpback whales sing songs that can last up to 35 minutes!

These harbor seals have a layer of fat, called blubber, under their skin to protect them from the cold.

FORESTS IN GLACIER BAY

The mostly trail-free wilderness of Glacier Bay is covered in thick forests. Among the evergreen trees, moose, brown and black bears, wolves, and mountain goats thrive in their natural habitat.

THE FACTS

Size: 3,281,789 acres (13,280.93 km²)
Highest point: 15,325 ft (4,671 m) at Mount Fairweather
Visitors each year: More than 600,000

Liverworts are similar to moss but wetter and live on the waterline of the bay.

The red parts of the Indian paintbrush found in the park are not flowers—they are leaves, called bracts.

23

TIDEWATER GLACIER

Johns Hopkins Glacier is 12 miles (19 km) long. It is one of seven tidewater glaciers found in Glacier Bay National Park and Preserve. Tidewater glaciers flow down to the sea. Other glaciers in the park remain in the mountains or melt before reaching the sea.

YELLOWSTONE

IDAHO–MONTANA–WYOMING ESTABLISHED 1872

Yellowstone was the first ever park to be given national park status. It is mostly untouched wilderness that is striking in its colorful beauty. Situated above a massive, dormant volcano, the park has many geothermal features—caused by underground heat.

Phlox flowers grow in the park's meadows from May through July.

Old Faithful is a geyser. It erupts about 17 times a day.

WONDERS OF WATER

There are more than 10,000 geothermal features in Yellowstone. Heated water rises through cracks in the ground, forming hot springs, geysers, steam vents, and bubbling mud pots. Together, they create a constantly changing landscape and may erupt into life at any moment!

PARK HABITATS

- 🔺 **Mountain**
- 🔺 **Tundra**
- ﹏ **Grassland**
- 🌲 **Coniferous forest**

Yellowstone supports more wildlife than any other park in the Lower 48 states. Many animals live in the mountains, forests, and grasslands. Microbes known as thermophiles even live in the Grand Prismatic Spring.

The **petrified trees** are a snapshot of prehistoric volcanic activity.

ABSAROKA RANGE

This mountain range on the park's eastern side is named for the Absaroka people of southern Montana. Many animals, including bighorn sheep and grizzly bears come down from the mountains in winter to search for food.

The mountain range is about 160 miles (257 km) long.

Lodgepole pine trees and their cones are common in the park.

The park's Grand Prismatic Spring is named for its rainbow colors. It is the largest hot spring in the United States.

FACTS

Size: 2,219,791 acres (8,983.17 km²)
Highest point: 11,372 ft (3,466 m) at Eagle Peak
Visitors each year: More than 4 million

RED FOX

The red fox plays a key role in the natural food chains at Yellowstone. It feeds on smaller animals, such as voles, and is itself preyed on by larger animals, such as wolves.

KOBUK VALLEY

ALASKA ESTABLISHED 1980

Due to its remote location in Alaska's Brooks Range, Kobuk Valley is one of the least visited national parks. Visitors have to travel by foot, boat, small aircraft, snowmobile, or dogsled. Alaska Natives have lived here for 10,000 years, surviving on food that they hunt or gather.

THREE DUNE FIELDS

There are three dune fields in the park. The sand was made by the grinding movement of glaciers in the surrounding mountains over tens of thousands of years. The dunes sprout grasses, wildflowers, sedges, and wild rye.

An area of the park called **Onion Portage** is named for the wild onions that grow there.

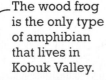

The wood frog is the only type of amphibian that lives in Kobuk Valley.

PARK HABITATS

- Desert
- Coniferous forest
- River
- Mountain

This park is centered around rare Arctic sand dunes that were formed during the last Ice Age. Surrounding the dunes are tundra, forests, rivers, and mountains—home to many animals.

The yellow-billed loon is one of the rarest birds that breeds in the States.

KOBUK LOCOWEED

In June and July, purple-pink Kobuk locoweed flowers in the dunes and surrounding forests. This plant grows wild only in Kobuk Valley.

FACTS

Size: 1,750,716 acres (7,084.90 km²)
Highest point: 4,629 ft (1,411 m) at Mount Angayukaqsraq
Visitors each year: Almost 16,000

CARIBOU MIGRATION

Twice a year, many thousands of caribou pass through the Kobuk Valley to and from their seasonal breeding grounds. Traditionally, Alaska Natives, called Nunamiut, used to follow and hunt the caribou on their journeys.

29

EVERGLADES

FLORIDA ESTABLISHED 1947

The Everglades is one of the world's largest tropical wetlands. It connects fresh water with salt water from the Gulf of Mexico and provides a home to a wide variety of plants and animals, especially birds. Its name is made up of the words "ever," from "forever," and "glades," meaning "grassy, open spaces."

THE FACTS

Size: 1,508,939 acres (6,106.46 km²)
Highest point: About 8 ft (2.4 m) in slash pine forest
Visitors each year: About 1.1 million

Saw grass is the most common plant found in the Everglades.

GRASSY WATERS

Saw grass marshes spread across the Everglades. They provide a home for many wildlife species. Seminole people, who still live in Florida, named the Everglades area Pa-hay-Okee, which means "grassy waters" in their language.

LIVING TOGETHER

This park is the only place where alligators and crocodiles share a home. Alligators prefer freshwater wetlands, while crocodiles can live in both fresh and salt water.

American alligator

American crocodile

PARK HABITATS

- **Wetland**
- **Tropical forest**
- **Mangrove**
- **Grassland**

This park is mostly wetlands, which include saw grass marshes, swamps, and wet prairies, as well as mangroves. Tropical forest also provides a home to wildlife, as do the park's estuaries.

Opossums are marsupials, distantly related to possums and other marsupials in Australia.

Opossums live in the park. The young often ride on their mother's back.

SHOREBIRDS

Sixteen species of shorebirds, such as the white ibis, live in the Everglades. They use their long beaks to probe for prey in shallow water.

The white ibis's favorite food is crayfish.

The brightly colored American purple gallinule lives in the Everglades.

GRAND CANYON

ARIZONA ESTABLISHED 1919

Carved by the mighty Colorado River over millions of years, the Grand Canyon is easily the most well-known ravine on Earth. The canyon and surrounding park stretch out beneath bright blue skies and puffy white clouds, and are filled with colorful rocks and desert vegetation.

PEOPLE OF THE CANYON

The Havasupai people have lived in this area for about 800 years. The Supai village, where the Havasupai still live, can be visited but hikers must be ready for a long journey through the desert to get there.

CALIFORNIA CONDOR

The park is home to one of the rarest birds in the world. There are only about 300 California condors in the wild, so it is said that seeing one is good luck.

Powerful beaks help these birds tear meat from dead animals.

THE FACTS

Size: 1,201,647 acres (4,862.89 km²),
6,093 ft (1,857 m) deep
Highest point: 8,803 ft (2,683 m)
at Point Imperial
Visitors each year:
About 6 million

PRICKLY PEAR CACTUS

There are many types of prickly pear cactus found in the park. Most live and grow on the inside of the dry, rocky canyon, and they provide bursts of bright yellow, red, or purple when they flower.

PARK HABITATS

🌵 **Desert**

〜 **River**

🌲 **Coniferous forest**

〰 **Grassland**

Most areas of the park are desert. In summer, temperatures can reach 120°F (49°C)! In higher areas, there are pine and spruce forests, and also patches of grassland. The river provides a home to fish and amphibians.

BIGHORN SHEEP

Using large horns that together can weigh up to 30 lb (14 kg), adult male bighorn sheep battle for mating rights. When fighting, they stand on their back legs and hurl themselves at each other. The clash of horns echoes through the canyon.

ANCIENT VALLEY

The layers of rock in the Grand Canyon began to form even before

dinosaurs were around! The Colorado Plateau, where the canyon

is found, started being pushed up about 70 million years ago.

Then, about 6 million years ago, the Colorado River

began to wear away the rock to create the steep-sided

valley that we see today.

GLACIER

MONTANA ESTABLISHED 1910

Called the "Crown of the Continent," Glacier was named for its slow rivers of ice—or glaciers—high in the granite mountain peaks. This park is known for its wildlife, including grizzly bears and mountain goats; clean lakes; and adventurous hiking trails.

Mountain goats live high up in the park.

THE FACTS

Size: 1,013,126 acres (4,099.98 km²)
Highest point: 10,466 ft (3,190 m) at Mount Cleveland
Visitors each year: More than 3 million

MELTING GLACIERS

Sadly, the glaciers in Glacier National Park are shrinking—only 35 remain. This shrinkage is expected to continue as temperatures rise due to climate change, which is causing summer melting to be greater than winter snowfalls.

GOING-TO-THE-SUN ROAD

Nearly 50 miles (80 km) of mountain road bring visitors across the Continental Divide and Logan Pass, where there are views of grand peaks in every direction. The iconic road was built in 1933.

OLYMPIC

WASHINGTON ESTABLISHED 1938

Split into three sections crossing coastal beach, tangled forests, and the glacier-capped Olympic Mountains, Olympic is a wonderland filled with amazing views and a variety of wildlife. The park and mountains take their name from Olympus—the mythical home of the Greek gods.

WILDLIFE

The Olympic mountains and moss-covered temperate rainforests are home to elk, mountain lions, black bears, and bobcats. The coastal waters provide a habitat for seals, sea lions, whales, and dolphins. The park has about 300 species of birds.

Old Man Stone at Ruby Beach teems with colonies of nesting birds.

PREHISTORIC LIFE

In the past 100 years, archaeologists have uncovered many clues about prehistoric life in the region. The remains of a mastodon from about 12,000–6,000 BCE were unearthed just outside the park in 1977.

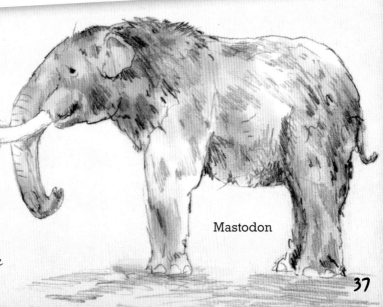

Mastodon

37

MOUNTAINS IN THE PARKS

The two national parks contain many mountains, including the Hermit (right) in Kings Canyon. However, Sequoia boasts Mount Whitney, which at 14,505 ft (4,421 m) is the highest of any peak in the United States, excluding Alaska.

SEQUOIA AND KINGS CANYON

CALIFORNIA ESTABLISHED 1890

Sequoia and Kings Canyon are two separate national parks that are run as a single park. Together, these parks are known as the "Land of Giants," and they are home to the world's largest trees; huge canyons; high mountain peaks; and many caves, meadows, and waterfalls.

COOL CAVES

There are about 275 caves in Sequoia and Kings Canyon. Some are wet and some are dry. They provide a home to many creatures, including bats, snakes, and insects.

SAVING FROGS

The numbers of yellow-legged frogs in the park began to fall when non-native fish species were introduced into their waters. The fish are now being removed to help the frog populations survive.

THE FACTS

Size: 865,964 acres (3504.43 km²)
Highest Point: 14,505 ft (4,421 m) at Mount Whitney
Vistors each year: Almost 1.9 million

Rare **bat species** live in the parks, such as Townsend's big-eared bat.

Sequoia groves are surrounded by meadows, lakes, rivers, and canyons of granite rock, where animals make their homes. Hardier animals tough it out in the mountain wilderness.

Giant sequoia tree leaves and cone

GENERAL SHERMAN TREE

This iconic giant sequoia tree is the largest living tree on Earth. It is ancient— between 2,300 and 2,700 years old. A trail takes visitors through the Giant Forest of sequoia trees and leads to the mighty trunk of the General Sherman.

BIG BEND

TEXAS ESTABLISHED 1944

Big Bend, named for the "big bend" in the Rio Grande, is a huge national park in the Chihuahuan Desert. It is home to unique wildlife, prehistoric geology, historical ruins, and rugged landscapes. Far from any city, the park is an amazing place to see stars twinkling endlessly in the night sky.

THE FACTS

Size: 801,163 acres (3,242.20 km²)
Highest point: 7,825 ft (2,385 m) at Emory Peak
Visitors each year: More than 450,000

RIO GRANDE

A 118-mile (190-km) stretch of the Rio Grande forms the southern border of the park. The river winds through dramatic canyons and the dry Chihuahuan Desert. It serves as a vital source of water for the desert plants and animals.

Black-tailed jackrabbits run in a zigzag to escape when being chased by predators, such as coyotes.

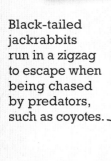

BIRDWATCHERS' PARADISE

Sitting along a key migration route, Big Bend is perfect for birdwatching. With more than 450 species, including the Mexican jay, vermilion flycatcher, and elf owl, Big Bend has more bird varieties than any other national park.

Big Bend is one of the best places to go **stargazing** since there is little light pollution.

Mexican jay

The giant dagger yucca blooms only when there has been enough rainfall.

FASCINATING FLORA

A wide variety of plant species, including cacti and yuccas, grows in the park. They store water in their stems and leaves, and often have sharp spines to deter plant-eaters.

PARK HABITATS

🌵 **Desert**

🔺 **Mountain**

🌲 **Coniferous forest**

〰️ **River**

Mainly desert, Big Bend also has mountain, forest, scrubland, and river habitats. The mighty Rio Grande is a magnet for much of the park's wildlife.

JOSHUA TREE

CALIFORNIA ESTABLISHED 1994

Mysterious and enchanting, Joshua Tree National Park may look bare, but it is filled with life. It is located where the Mojave and Colorado deserts meet. During the day, bright sun shines down on the sand, and, at night, the skies are filled with twinkling stars.

The rare Scott's oriole arrives at the park every year in spring and summer to nest.

THE FACTS

Size: 795,156 acres (3217.88 km²)
Highest point: 5,816 ft (1,773 m) at Quail Mountain
Visitors each year: About 3 million

JOSHUA TREES

The park is named for these unique plants that sprinkle the desert. However, Joshua trees aren't really trees at all, but tall yucca plants.

Joshua trees have spiky green leaves.

DESERT NIGHT LIZARD

Wildlife at Joshua Tree must cope with the hot desert environment. The desert night lizard lives under the fallen branches of Joshua trees, where it can hunt for insects while escaping the daytime heat.

A HOME TO MANY

Many different peoples have lived in the Joshua Tree region, including the Pinto culture, the Cahuilla, the Chemehuevi, the Serrano, ranchers, and miners. Rock carvings, called petroglyphs, can be found throughout the park.

PARK HABITATS

 Desert   Mountain

Joshua Tree crosses the Mojave and Colorado deserts. There are six mountain ranges in the park, and plants and animals are uniquely suited to the harsh, varying conditions.

STARGAZING

Southern California has plenty of light pollution, but not here — at Joshua Tree, visitors can see glittering stars, planets, and the Milky Way galaxy in some of the clearest skies in the region.

Ocotillo plants found in Joshua Tree have beautiful red flowers.

43

YOSEMITE

CALIFORNIA ESTABLISHED 1890

This national park is well known for its cascading waterfalls, huge cliffs, and deep valleys. Visitors are also drawn to Yosemite especially to see the legendary giant sequoia trees, which are among the tallest trees in the world.

Yosemite Falls

EL CAPITAN

Yosemite's cliffs inspire brave climbers. El Capitan is about 3,000 ft (914 m) at its tallest face. That's almost 10 times taller than the Statue of Liberty.

WATERFALLS

At a towering 2,425 ft (739 m), Yosemite Falls is one of the world's tallest waterfalls. It has three steps, made of smaller falls—Upper Yosemite Fall, the Middle Cascades, and Lower Yosemite Fall.

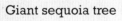

Giant sequoia tree

THE FACTS

Size: 761,748 acres (3,082.68 km²)
Highest point: 13,114 ft (3,997 m) at Mount Lyell
Visitors each year: More than 4 million

Giant sequoias are conifers with thin leaves and scaly cones.

PARK HABITATS

△ Mountain

🌲 Coniferous forest

〰 Grassland

〰 River

Yosemite's many habitats include grasslands, scrublands, and coniferous forests that surround the high granite peaks. This mixture provides for a wide variety of plants and animals.

HOME IN YOSEMITE

For thousands of years before modern settlers entered the Yosemite Valley, the Miwok people, and others, made their home in this area. They built cedar-bark shelters, called umachas, for protection from the weather.

BLACK BEARS

Yosemite is well known as the home of the majestic black bear. In fact, up to 500 black bears live in the park. Despite their name, many black bears have brown fur similar to their larger brown bear cousins, who are not found in this park.

KENAI FJORDS

ALASKA ESTABLISHED 1980

Alaska's smallest national park has a 545-mile (877-km) coastline of glacier-carved fjords—narrow strips of sea between tall cliffs. On shore, the icy glaciers tower over dense forests that are filled with wildlife.

Mountain goats can climb rocky cliffs that other animals can't.

HARDING ICEFIELD

The vast Harding Icefield contains about 40 glaciers that stretch as far as the eye can see. Glaciers are massive rivers of ice that slowly flow down mountains. The Aialik Glacier in Kenai flows into Aialik Bay.

BOATING AROUND

One of the best ways to see the icebergs, glaciers, and mountains of Kenai is by boat. Sea lions and whales may pop up to say hello, too!

THE FACTS

Size: 669,650 acres (2,709.98 km²)
Highest point: 6,612 ft (2,015 m) at Truuli Peak
Visitors each year: More than 300,000

46

ISLE ROYALE

MICHIGAN ESTABLISHED 1940

Isle Royale sits in the northwestern corner of Lake Superior. The park is made up of the isle and the hundreds of smaller islands around it. With no roads or towns, it is 99 percent wilderness and home to wolves, moose, and many other animals.

CROSSING THE LAKE

Visitors can only reach this park by boat or seaplane. In winter, when the lake sometimes freezes, the park is closed, but a few researchers still go there to study the animals.

SHIPWRECKS

Over the years, hundreds of boats have sunk in the wild waters off Isle Royale. Some visitors go scuba diving to explore the wrecks and spot some of the many types of fish found in the lake.

THE FACTS

Size: 571,790 acres (2,313.95 km²)
Highest point: 1,394 ft (425 m) at Mount Desor
Visitors each year: About 26,000

GREAT SMOKY MOUNTAINS

NORTH CAROLINA–TENNESSEE

ESTABLISHED 1934

As the United States' most visited national park, the Great Smoky Mountains welcomes more than 12.5 million visitors each year. Some come for adventure and many just travel through. Rivers call to paddlers, the Appalachian Trail beckons long-distance hikers, and the Cherokee have called the area home for millennia.

Fireflies light up the forests in early summer when they produce flashes to attract mates.

Clingmans Dome is the highest point in the park and has 360° views.

BLUE SMOKE

The Great Smokies got their name from the legendary blue haze that blankets the mountains. Cherokees called the region Shaconage, which means "place of blue smoke." The bluish color is a result of gases exhaled by plants mixing with fog.

THE FACTS

Size: 522,427 acres (2,114.19 km²)
Highest point: 6,643 ft (2,025 m) at Clingmans Dome
Visitors each year: More than 12.5 million

Marbled salamander

SALAMANDERS

The Great Smoky Mountains are known as the salamander capital of the world! Thirty species of these amphibians live there, including the marbled salamander and many lungless species.

These insects are called handsome fungus beetles. They feed on fungi under the bark of dead trees.

PARK HABITATS

Mountain

Deciduous forest

Coniferous forest

River

This park is dominated by the mountains, which are carpeted in deciduous and coniferous forests, and home to an abundance of wildlife. The streams and Little River support many animals, too.

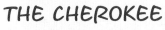

THE CHEROKEE

The Cherokee are known for their skills in hunting, farming, and trading goods. They have lived in the Great Smoky Mountains for about 4,000 years.

Red columbine grows on the forest floor.

THICKLY FORESTED

Evergreen trees such as firs and pines blanket the misty higher slopes of the Great Smoky Mountains National Park. Deciduous (leaf-shedding) trees, such as maples, beeches, and hickories, cover the lower regions.

NORTH CASCADES

WASHINGTON ESTABLISHED 1968

North Cascades National Park Complex is a landscape of dense ancient forests, brightly colored alpine lakes, giant glaciers, rugged mountains, and waterfalls. In this unique national park, there are almost 400 miles (644 km) of trails to follow, more than 500 lakes to explore, and many peaks to climb or admire from afar. Endless opportunities for adventure await!

Pikas live in the park. They may look like rodents, but they are closely related to rabbits.

DIABLO LAKE

This lake is a popular destination for canoeing and kayaking, and for just taking in the stunning views of the evergreen forests. Particles of rock from nearby glaciers flow into the lake, turning its water a rich turquoise.

MOUNT BAKER

This active volcano rises more than 10,781 ft (3,286 m) in the Cascade Mountain Range and overlooks the park. It is covered by 13 glaciers and is one of the snowiest mountains on Earth, making it a great place for downhill ski runs.

THE FACTS

Size: 504,781 acres (2,042.77 km²)
Highest point: 9,199 ft (2,804 m) at Goode Mountain
Visitors each year: More than 38,000

GLACIERS

There are more than 300 glaciers in the park, giving the mountains their snowcapped peaks. When they melt, the water cascades, or falls, down the mountains, producing the many waterfalls that the park is known for.

PARK HABITATS

 Coniferous forest

 Mountain

 River

Lake

Waterfalls flow from the Cascade Range's peaks, feeding the rivers and lakes and supplying the forests, hillsides, and meadows with vital water. These habitats support the park's thriving communities of animals.

Wild strawberries

SAVING NATIVE PLANTS

Native plants are essential to the park's ecosystem. However, they are often trampled by hikers. To protect the plants, rangers grow them in a safe environment and then reintroduce them to the park in fall.

The park is home to a small number of grizzly bears.

CANYONLANDS

UTAH ESTABLISHED 1964

Canyonlands is exactly how it sounds—a land of canyons! It is home to grand vistas of red rock, desert birds and animals, and some wonderful rock arches that were formed over millions of years. The Green and Colorado rivers wind through the canyons under the bold Utah sun, which colors the canyons.

FOUR DISTRICTS

The park has four districts: Island in the Sky, the Needles, the Maze, and the Green and Colorado rivers. Island in the Sky attracts the most visitors. The "island" is a flat-topped hill with steep sides that towers above its surroundings. This district also boasts many picturesque arches.

Yucca flowers are pollinated only by yucca moths.

SURVIVING IN THE DESERT

With little water to go around, the park's trees are spread far apart. Their roots can split rocks in search of water. In extreme times, the Utah juniper cuts off the water supply to its branches to help it survive.

Utah junipers often live longer than 700 years.

Size: 337,598 acres (1,366.21 km²)
Highest point: 7,120 ft (2,170 m)
at Cathedral Point
Visitors each year: More than 730,000

THE NEEDLES

The remote Needles district is dominated by colorful sandstone spires. There are more than 60 miles (97 km) of hiking trails and many off-road driving adventures that lead into backcountry areas.

Horseshoe Canyon has displays of ancient American Indian rock art.

Turkey vultures use their sharp eyesight and sense of smell to find food.

This artwork is known as the Holy Ghost panel.

PARK HABITATS

 Desert River

The high desert landscape at Canyonlands is made up of rock formations, mazes of canyons, and river corridors—only the most drought-tolerant plants and animals survive. The Colorado River and the lush vegetation on its banks attract a wealth of wildlife.

AMERICAN INDIAN ART

There are two types of ancient rock art in Canyonlands: petroglyphs, which are etchings carved into sandstone, and pictographs, which are paintings made with mineral pigments and plant dyes.

HAWAI'I VOLCANOES

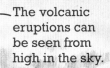

The volcanic eruptions can be seen from high in the sky.

HAWAI'I ESTABLISHED 1916

Erupting with sea, sun, and tropical wildlife, Hawai'i Volcanoes National Park is a magical world. Formed around two active volcanoes, this national park has a landscape sculpted by fire. It's no wonder that Hawai'i Volcanoes is believed to be the home of Pele, the goddess of fire, and is sacred to Hawaiians and legendary in Polynesian culture.

ACTIVE VOLCANOES

Hawai'i Volcanoes is named for the two lava-filled mountains that are in the park. One is Kīlauea—one of the world's most active volcanoes—which last erupted between 1983 and 2018. The other is Mauna Loa, which if measured from its top in the sky to its bottom in the ocean, is taller than Mount Everest!

THE LEHUA FLOWER

The 'ōhi'a lehua flower is the first plant to grow after entire regions are covered with lava. With its smoldering colors, this plant is associated with the Hawaiian fire goddess, Pele.

Yellow lehua flowers have long, broad, pointed leaves.

PARK HABITATS

- **Mountain**
- **Tropical forest**
- **Coast**

Hawai'i was created by volcanic activity and is the only US state with tropical rainforest—a habitat for many animals. Beaches provide nesting sites for turtles.

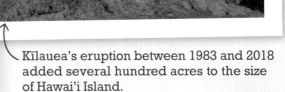

Kīlauea's eruption between 1983 and 2018 added several hundred acres to the size of Hawai'i Island.

Volcanic rock

Mauna Loa broke through the surface of the Pacific Ocean almost half a million years ago, and it's still growing today.

THE FACTS

Size: 325,605 acres (1,317.68 km^2)
Highest point: 13,678 ft (4,169 m) at Mauna Loa
Visitors each year: About 1.37 million

THE STATE BIRD

The Hawaiian goose, or nēnē, is under threat. Predators and human land development threaten its existence, so it's a protected species.

VOLCANIC LANDSCAPE

The living, breathing volcanoes in Hawai'i Volcanoes National Park are unsettled, wild, and unpredictable. Their eruptions have created a vast, rocky landscape, which has many volcanic features, such as lava tubes, moonlike craters, and steam vents.

GRAND TETON

WYOMING ESTABLISHED 1929

Grand Teton and the other mountains in the Teton Range are the youngest in the Rockies—they started to form nine million years ago. Their jagged peaks rise 7,000 ft (2,134 m) from the valley floor of Jackson Hole, Wyoming. They tower over mirrored lakes and the Snake River, where wildlife makes its home.

PARK WILDLIFE

Grand Teton National Park attracts a wealth of wildlife. Mammals range from huge bison, grizzly bears, and moose (opposite), to voles and shrews. Birds in the park include bald eagles and calliope hummingbirds. Reptiles, amphibians, fish, and countless invertebrates, such as insects, live here too.

THE FACTS

Size: 310,044 acres (1,254.70 km²)
Highest point: 13,775 ft (4,199 m) at Grand Teton
Visitors each year: About 3.4 million

SHEEPEATERS

The Shoshone people in the region were known as "Sheepeaters," because they hunted bighorn sheep, which live on the high slopes. The sheep's horns were made into tools, and every other part of the animal was used or eaten.

Mountaineers come from all over the world to climb the three Tetons: Grand, Middle, and South.

Traditionally, the Shoshone lived in tepees.

PARK HABITATS

 Mountain

 Deciduous forest

 Coniferous forest

 Lake

The mountains are the dominant feature in Grand Teton. They look down onto the other habitats, including forests, lakes, rivers, scrublands, and wetlands. Such a varied landscape supports a wide range of animal populations.

Female moose are called cows. They care for their calves for about a year.

MOOSE

There are many moose in the park. The largest of the deer family, they find refuge in the woods, meadows, lakes, and streams. In fall, their mating calls echo across the landscape.

Oxbow Bend is a curved section of the Snake River.

ROCKY MOUNTAIN

COLORADO ESTABLISHED 1915

This popular national park is called Rocky Mountain for a good reason! Its jagged peaks and steep mountain trails draw in thousands of mountaineers and hikers every year—but many of the routes are not for the fainthearted. The park is also home to beautiful meadows; dense forests; and glistening rivers, lakes, and glaciers.

The **red crossbill** has an unusual crossed beak for eating seeds from conifer cones

The Keyhole rock formation is found on Longs Peak.

LONGS PEAK

The highest mountain in the park, Longs Peak, is so tall that it can be seen from miles away. Made of light-gray granite, this mighty mountain is loved by hikers and mountaineers.

THE FACTS

Size: 265,807 acres (1,075.68 km²)
Highest point: 14,259 ft (4,346 m) at Longs Peak
Visitors each year: About 4.5 million

TRAIL RIDGE ROAD

Nicknamed the "Highway to the Sky," this road takes visitors up to 12,183 ft (3,713 m) through pine forests and wildflower meadows. Linking the towns of Estes Park and Grand Lake, Trail Ridge Road has a stunning view of the park.

← Oxeye daisies grow in the park.

PARK HABITATS

 Mountain

 Coniferous forest

 Grassland

In the lower areas of the park, meadow valleys and slopes support animal populations. In the higher areas, evergreen forests climb up the sides of the mountains.

MOUNTAIN LION

These powerful cats are skilled hunters. While stalking prey, such as deer, they hide behind trees and boulders, then pounce when least expected. Also known as pumas or cougars, mountain lions usually like to keep their distance from humans.

BEAR LAKE

This alpine lake is a popular destination in Rocky Mountain National Park. It was created by a glacier in the distant past and sits below the 12,598-ft- (3,840-m-) high Hallett Peak. A trail around the lake takes hikers through a coniferous forest, home to chickadees, squirrels, elk, and many more animals.

CHANNEL ISLANDS

CALIFORNIA ESTABLISHED 1980

The Channel Islands lie off the coast of southern California. This island chain is home to plants, animals, birds, and marine life found nowhere else in the world. There is also a lively community of marine animals, living among and around the seagrass beds and seaweed forests.

THE FACTS

Size: 249,561 acres (1,009.94 km²)
Highest point: 2,450 ft (747 m) at Devils Peak
Visitors each year: More than 400,000

THE ISLANDS

There are eight islands that make up the Channel Islands chain. Five of them form the national park: Anacapa, Santa Cruz, Santa Rosa, San Miguel, and Santa Barbara islands. Each of the islands has its own unique character and wildlife.

Giant coreopsis grows in the park. It has bright yellow flowers and sturdy treelike stems.

ISLAND WILDLIFE

The park has more than 2,000 plant and animal species. The islands even have their own species of fox—simply called the island fox. The coastal waters abound with sea life such as sunflower stars, sea lions, and whales.

About 80,000 California sea lions breed on the park's San Miguel Island.

PARK HABITATS

Ocean

Coast

Grassland

Scrubland

The islands' coastlines and surrounding ocean are incredibly rich in many forms of life. Onshore, grassland, scrubland, and forest provide a home to many animals.

THE CHUMASH

Humans have lived on the Channel Islands for at least 13,000 years. The Chumash people are the most famous inhabitants. Their name translates as "makers of shell bead money."

The Chumash built boats, called tomols, which they used for fishing and trading goods.

BADLANDS

SOUTH DAKOTA ESTABLISHED 1978

Named by the Lakota people for its extreme temperatures and rough landscape, Badlands feature hills, canyons, and rocky pinnacles. These impressive formations are made up of layers of rock that have worn down over time, revealing the colorful striped rocks we can see today.

In 1979, the **black-footed ferret** was declared extinct, but it was rediscovered in 1981,

THE FACTS

Size: 242,756 acres (982.39 km²)
Highest point: 3,340 ft (1,018 m)
at Red Shirt Table
Visitors each year:
About 1 million

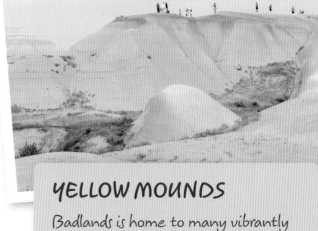

YELLOW MOUNDS

Badlands is home to many vibrantly colored rocks. The Yellow Mounds are made of bright yellow fossil soil, called paleosol, and they contain fossils of prehistoric sea creatures.

AMERICAN BISON

The largest mammal in the United States, the American bison is easily spotted roaming the Badlands. Bison are protected because their numbers plummeted in the 19th century due to hunting, but populations are slowly recovering.

CAPITOL REEF

Apples

UTAH ESTABLISHED 1971

Named for the white domes of sandstone, which look like the domes of the capitol buildings found throughout the United States, Capitol Reef is filled with stunning and strangely shaped rock formations. In summer, temperatures here can reach a baking 100°F (38°C).

THE FACTS

Size: 241,905 acres (978.95 km²)
Highest point: 8,960 ft (2,731 m) at the Colorado Plateau
Visitors each year: More than 1.2 million

FRUITA DISTRICT

Fruita was established in 1880. No more than 10 families ever lived there at one time. It was named for its many orchards, where apples, pears, cherries, and other fruits were grown. Farming in this hot area was only possible near the Fremont River.

WATERPOCKET FOLD

Almost 100 miles (161 km) long, the Waterpocket Fold is a "wrinkle" in the Earth's surface. Between 50 and 70 million years ago, movements of the Earth's crust pushed up a section of land that is now 7,000 ft (2,133 m) higher to the west.

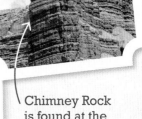

Chimney Rock is found at the edge of the Waterpocket Fold.

MOUNT RAINIER

WASHINGTON ESTABLISHED 1899

This active stratovolcano is an icon in Washington State. The park containing it is filled with glaciers, thick forests, and fields of wildflowers. Rainier and its surrounding mountains are part of the Cascade Range, and their snowy peaks dominate the landscape.

The park is home to hundreds of wildflower species, such as this scarlet paintbrush.

WILDFLOWER MEADOWS

The park is known for colorful displays of beautiful wildflowers, such as purple broadleaf lupines, in summer. Flowers that can cope with shade grow in the park's forests, while flowers that need plenty of sunshine thrive in the mountain meadows.

RESTORING FISHERS

Fishers are relatives of weasels that were once wiped out in Washington due to overhunting for their valuable fur. They are now being reintroduced to their native habitat and can be found nesting in hollow trees in the park's forests.

Harlequin ducks fly to the park in spring to nest.

PARK HABITATS

🌲 **Coniferous forest**

〰️ **Grassland**

⛰️ **Mountain**

🏔️ **Snow and ice**

Volcanoes, mountains, and glaciers tower above all else in this park. Evergreen forests roll down to grassland meadows, where many animals make their homes.

The Tatoosh Range, found in the park and the adjacent wilderness, is part of the Cascades.

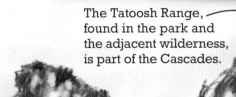

REFLECTION LAKES

One of the best views of Mount Rainier is at the Reflection Lakes. On a clear, still day, the volcano is reflected perfectly in the waters of these mountain pools.

THE FACTS

Size: 236,382 acres (956.60 km²)
Highest point: 14,411 ft (4,392 m) at Mount Rainier
Visitors each year: About 1.5 million

PETRIFIED FOREST

ARIZONA ESTABLISHED 1962

Filled with rainbow landscapes and open spaces, this park's treasure is an ancient forest. It's made up of one of the world's largest collections of 225-million-year-old petrified wood (wood that has turned to stone). The giant fossilized logs are filled with colorful quartz rock. All around them are dinosaur fossils.

PAINTED DESERT

The Painted Desert was given its name by Spanish explorers. They thought the clay and mudstone looked like a sunset painted onto the landscape. At the Painted Desert Inn, murals offer a glimpse into the culture of one of the desert's first peoples, the Hopi.

THE FACTS

Size: 221,390 acres (895.93 km^2)
Highest point: 6,224 ft (1,897 m) at Pilot Rock
Visitors each year: Almost 650,000

PARK HABITATS

🌵 **Desert**

〰️ **Grassland**

🌿 **Scrubland**

🌲 **Coniferous forest**

The park is located in a high desert region, but it also has shortgrass prairies, scrubland, and coniferous forests. All these habitats support a diverse range of mammals, reptiles, birds, and other animals.

THE PUEBLO PEOPLE

A thousand years ago, the Pueblo people lived and farmed in the Petrified Forest area. They used stone from petrified wood to build their "pueblos" (houses) and made many carvings, called petroglyphs, in rocks (above).

Collared lizards live in the park. They prey on insects, spiders, and other reptiles.

GOPHER SNAKE

Common in the park, these nonvenomous snakes may imitate rattlesnakes by hissing, vibrating their tails, and striking when threatened.

Steller's jay is a blue and black bird that can mimic the calls of many other birds and animals.

QUARTZ LOGS

These rock fossils are the remains of prehistoric trees that were buried deep underground. Movement of the Earth's tectonic plates pushed the fossils to the surface, broken up into chunks.

VOYAGEURS

MINNESOTA ESTABLISHED 1975

This Minnesotan park borders Canada and is a watery wonderland of lakes. Its rich landscape also includes forests, marshes, and bogs. The park was named for the "voyageurs"—French-Canadian fur traders who explored the region in canoes with the help of the Ojibwe people.

FACTS

Size: 218,222 acres (883.11 km²)
Highest point: 1,410 ft (430 m) at an unnamed point
Visitors each year: Almost 235,000

Maple leaves

NUMEROUS LAKES

The park contains four large lakes, called Rainy Lake, Kabetogama, Namakan, and Sand Point, and many other smaller lakes. About one-third of the park is covered by water.

Kabetogama's shape was carved by a glacier thousands of years ago. Today, its waters are crystal clear.

THE CRY OF THE LOON

The common loon has an eerie call, which echoes over the lakes. Minnesota has the largest loon population in the Lower 48 states.

SHENANDOAH

VIRGINIA ESTABLISHED 1935

American Indians, miners, loggers, soldiers, and explorers have all traveled through the Blue Ridge Mountains. These mountains are also home to the Shenandoah National Park, which is filled with beautiful waterfalls, streams, and wooded hollows.

FACTS

Size: 199,224 acres (806.23 km²)
Highest point: 4,051 ft (1,235 m) at Hawksbill Mountain
Visitors each year: About 1.4 million

SKYLINE DRIVE

This 105-mile (169-km) scenic road runs the full length of Shenandoah. It winds its way past rolling hills, historic houses, and sturdy mountains, and is the only public road through the park.

Hickory trees have delicate blossoms and large nuts.

Milkweed blooms in summer. Its pink flowers attract monarch butterflies.

The **scarlet tanager** is brightly colored and lives high up in trees.

WILDFLOWERS ABOUND

Flowers blossom most of the year in the park, creating kaleidoscopes of color. Spring is the best time to see them—when nearly 900 species bloom in the meadows and forests.

CRATER LAKE

OREGON ESTABLISHED 1902

The main attraction of Crater Lake National Park is its namesake—Crater Lake. It was created 7,700 years ago when a massive volcano erupted and collapsed, forming the deep crater that is now filled with water. The lake is known for its pure, clear, bright-blue water, which is fed by rainfall and snowmelt.

"The Old Man" is a floating tree stump that has been bobbing in the water for 100 years.

WIZARD ISLAND

This island is a volcano that has risen from Crater lake. Some of the trees that grow on its slopes are about 800 years old. The island is so named because it looks like a wizard's hat!

THE FACTS

Size: 183,224 acres (741.48 km²)
Highest point: 8,929 ft (2,721 m) at Mount Scott
Visitors each year: More than 700,000

Cyclists can ride around the 33-mile (53-km) rim of Crater Lake.

PHANTOM SHIP ISLAND

This tiny island in Crater Lake looks like a phantom ship adrift in the cold water. It is made of volcanic rock that is more than 400,000 years old.

Golden-mantled ground squirrels are noticeable in the park because they are bold in color and friendly around humans.

PARK HABITATS

 Lake

 Mountain

 Coniferous forest

The park lies in the heart of the Cascade Range and is surrounded by forests. At its center, Crater Lake is home to aquatic animals.

SCIENCE AND LEARNING CENTER

The lake is a living laboratory filled with natural wonders. The scientists and researchers who come to study the lake can stay in this renovated house during their visits.

DEEP WATERS

Crater Lake contains 4.6 trillion gallons (17.4 trillion liters) of water. Its maximum depth is 1,943 ft (592 m), making it the deepest lake in the United States and the ninth deepest on Earth. When a group of explorers came across the lake in 1833, while searching for gold, they named it Deep Blue Lake. It was renamed Crater Lake in 1869.

BISCAYNE

FLORIDA ESTABLISHED 1980

Off the shores of Miami lies a national park that can only be explored by sea. With beautiful coral reefs and mangrove forests, Biscayne is the perfect place to see an amazing variety of marine animals, from sea turtles and lobsters to manatees and dolphins.

THE FACTS

Size: 172,971 acres (699.99 km²)
Highest point: 9 ft (3 m) at Totten Key and Old Rhodes Key
Visitors each year: More than 700,000

BISCAYNE BAY

The lagoons at Biscayne Bay are popular with divers. There are many marine animals to see, including corals, parrotfish, butterflyfish, angelfish, and sea turtles. Divers can follow a set route underwater—the Maritime Heritage Trail.

The Maritime Heritage Trail features six shipwrecks.

MANATEES

These gentle giants are also known as "sea cows" because they are large, slow-moving animals that graze on seagrass. Florida manatees can be spotted from November to April in the park, but they are vulnerable to collisions with boats.

Mangrove flowers bloom during the spring and summer months.

Manatees have paddle-shaped tails.

PARK HABITATS

Coral reef

Mangrove

Ocean

Coast

Biscayne Bay's large estuary— where fresh and salt water meet—is a haven to coral communities and mangrove trees. Aquatic and land animals come together here, too.

MANGROVE FORESTS

Leafy mangrove trees live half above the sea and half below. Just 1 acre (4,050 m²) of mangroves can shed up to 3 tons (2.7 tonnes) of leaves per year, making them an important food source for fish, worms, and crustaceans.

Fowey Rocks Lighthouse stands 110 ft (33.5 m) above water.

81

GREAT SAND DUNES

NATIONAL PARK & PRESERVE

COLORADO ESTABLISHED 2004

Great Sand Dunes National Park and Preserve is home to the highest dune field in North America. The huge peaks of sand cover roughly 19,200 acres (78 km²). The park's tallest dune is named Star Dune. It is 755 ft (230 m) high from its base to its top—that's more than twice as tall as the Statue of Liberty!

THE FACTS

Size: 149,028 acres (603 km²)
Highest point: 13,604 ft (4,146 m) at Tijeras Peak
Visitors each year: More than 500,000

Pronghorn live in the grasslands and can run at speeds of more than 50 mph (80 kph).

ANCIENT SAND

The dune field at Great Sand Dunes stretches as far as the eye can see. The sand is made up of 29 different types of minerals, such as turquoise and amethyst, and the sand itself is roughly 35 million years old!

On cloudless, moonless nights, campers in the park can see thousands of stars in the sky.

WETLANDS

The park is dotted with wetlands. They are vital for animals, including elk, shorebirds, and dragonflies, during the scorching summers. They can freeze over in winter.

About 20,000 sandhill cranes make their way through the park in spring and fall.

The Great Sand Dunes tiger beetle is found only in this park.

TIGER BEETLE

The park is home to the Great Sand Dunes tiger beetle. At just ¾ in (2 cm) long, these bugs have green and blue metallic heads and beautiful violin-shaped markings on their wing cases. They can live for about two and a half years.

Prairie sunflowers brighten up the grasslands and dunes in summer.

PARK HABITATS

🌵 **Desert**

⛰ **Mountain**

〰 **Grassland**

🌱 **Scrubland**

The dune field is surrounded by grasslands and wetlands that are fed by life-sustaining creeks. The park's mountains and scrublands also support a wealth of wildlife.

BREATHTAKING DUNES

The huge dunes of Great Sand Dunes National Park and Preserve sit beneath the peaks of the Sangre de Cristo Mountains. Two streams flowing from the mountains deposit sand around the dune field. The wind then blows this sand onto the dunes.

ZION

UTAH ESTABLISHED 1919

Utah's first national park lies where the Great Basin, the Colorado Plateau, and the Mojave Desert all meet. Its dramatic landscape was created over millions of years by water, wind, and ice. Its famous canyons were home to the Anasazi and Paiute people until Mormon settlers came to the area in the 1860s.

THE FACTS

Size: 147,243 acres (595.87 km^2)
Highest point: 8,726 ft (2,660 m) at Horse Ranch Mountain
Visitors each year: Almost 4.5 million

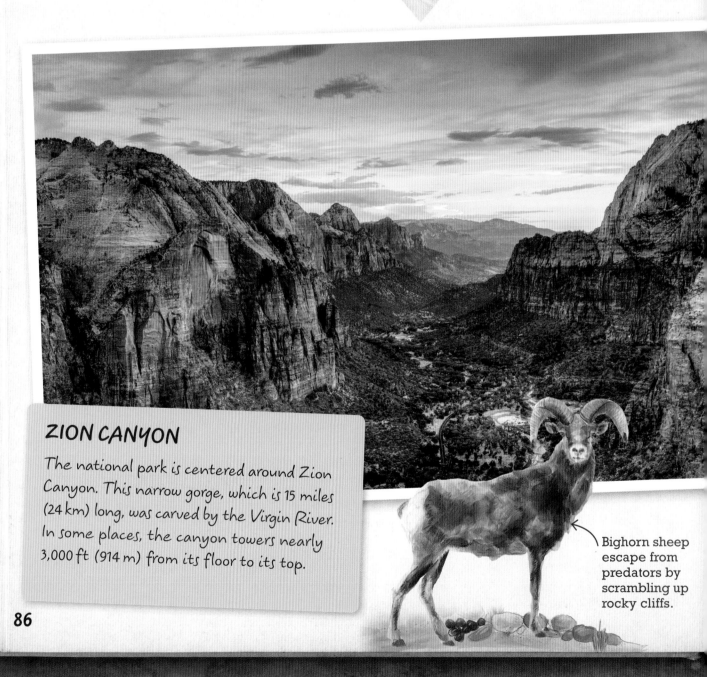

ZION CANYON

The national park is centered around Zion Canyon. This narrow gorge, which is 15 miles (24 km) long, was carved by the Virgin River. In some places, the canyon towers nearly 3,000 ft (914 m) from its floor to its top.

Bighorn sheep escape from predators by scrambling up rocky cliffs.

JUNIOR PARK RANGER

Young explorers in Zion, and many other national parks, can become Junior Rangers and earn a badge by completing activities. These fun pursuits include hiking and solving puzzles.

MEXICAN SPOTTED OWL

This skilled hunter survives in the shade of the red rock canyons. The species is under threat elsewhere due to loss of habitat, but it has found protection in the park.

Zion is a great place for scientists to study Earth's prehistoric past.

PARK HABITATS

⬔ **Mountain**

✿ **Desert**

≋ **River**

🌲 **Coniferous forest**

Coniferous forests and desert-adapted plants dot the slopes of the mountains in this park. Hidden within the canyon mazes are many springs and waterfalls that act as magnets to wildlife.

The park's Kayenta and Moenave rock layers contain fossils of **dinosaur tracks.**

FOSSIL-HUNTING KIT

Scientists who study fossils use a variety of tools to find and extract them carefully from the surrounding rock.

A magnifying glass can show the finer details of a fossil.

WHITE SANDS

NEW MEXICO ESTABLISHED 2019

Stark, powdery dunes make the landscape at White Sands National Park look like the surface of an alien planet. This part of the Chihuahuan Desert in southern New Mexico is home to sprawling dunes that stretch away beneath the vast, starry skies.

Desert mentzelia has bright-yellow flowers that look like stars. It is also called stickleaf.

BLENDING IN

The bleached earless lizard is so pale that it blends in with the surrounding gypsum sand. This camouflage protects it from predators.

THE FACTS

Size: 146,344 acres (592.23 km^2)
Highest point: 4,116 ft (1,255 m) at a former military site called NE 30
Visitors each year: More than 600,000

Bleached earless lizard

SLEDDING ON THE SANDS

Adventurous people visit the park for a special thrill—to sled down the soft slopes of gypsum sand. The sleds are large saucers that are waxed to reduce friction. It may take a few rides to master this fun way of sledding!

REDWOOD

CALIFORNIA ESTABLISHED 1968

Redwood National and State Parks are home to the tallest trees on Earth. These ancient trees create a mystical canopy where flying squirrels and countless birds find shelter near the California coast. Large herds of Roosevelt elk roam shady clearings within the woods.

Western meadowlarks are songbirds that live in the oak woods and open grasslands of the park.

COAST REDWOOD

Coast redwoods can grow to almost 400 ft (122 m) tall. Their strong root systems help them survive storms and floods. Because of this, some are more than 2,000 years old. This magnificent species has existed for about 240 million years.

Trillium has white or pink flowers and grows under coast redwoods.

ORCAS

Also known as killer whales, orcas are seen off the park's coast all year. They are especially attracted to the area in August and September by migrating Chinook salmon.

THE FACTS

Size: 138,999 acres (562.51 km²)
Highest point: 3,170 ft (966 m) at Coyote Peak
Visitors each year: More than 500,000

LASSEN VOLCANIC

CALIFORNIA ESTABLISHED 1916

Volcanoes, lakes, meadows, waterfalls, and streams all coexist in this wild environment, providing a happy home to wildlife. Steam vents, mud pots, geysers, and hot springs are some of the geothermal features of this park. They bubble up from the ground, creating a volcanic wonderland.

HIKING TO LASSEN PEAK

Lassen Peak is the highest peak in the park. This mountain gave the park its name. Visitors must hike for 2.5 miles (4 km) and climb a further 2,000 ft (610 m) to get to its summit.

Campers on long trips can discover hidden lakes.

SIERRA NEVADA RED FOX

The Sierra Nevada red fox lives high in the Cascades and Sierra Nevada mountains. Its numbers are dwindling, probably due to trapping, habitat loss, climate change, and competition from other predators.

90

THE FACTS

Size: 106,589 acres (431.35 km²)
Highest point: 10,457 ft (3,187 m)
at Lassen Peak
Visitors each year:
More than 500,000

A FORESTED PARK

Most of the park is covered in forest, and it neighbors the vast Lassen National Forest. Filled with red fir and cottonwood, the forests provide a habitat for animals, including mule deer and mountain lions.

Lassen's red firs can stand 175 ft (53 m) tall and live for 300 years!

PARK HABITATS

⛰ **Mountain**

🏞 **Lake**

🌲 **Coniferous forest**

〰 **Grassland**

Coniferous forests creep up the sides of the park's volcanoes. There are grasslands, too, and the landscape is dotted with lakes, making it an ideal home for wildlife, including a small population of black bears.

Subway Cave is a lava tube—a tunnel that was made by flowing molten rock—near the park.

In fall, gold-colored aspen leaves stand out against the evergreens.

SAGUARO

ARIZONA ESTABLISHED 1994

Saguaro National Park is divided into two districts. The Rincon Mountain District in the east is mountainous and wild with high desert forests and shy wildlife. The western Tucson Mountain District is red rock desert with tall cacti reaching into sunny blue skies.

GILA MONSTER

This reptile is one of only two venomous lizards in North America. Gila monsters spend almost all of their time underground, making them very hard to spot.

A Saguaro cactus produces up to 100 flowers each spring.

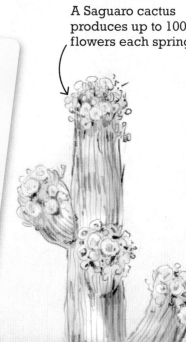

SAGUARO CACTUS

The park was named for the Saguaro cactus. It's the largest species of cactus in the United States. Standing tall with "arms" curving upward, this noble-looking plant has been nicknamed the "desert monarch."

GUADALUPE MOUNTAINS

TEXAS ESTABLISHED 1972

Home of the highest peaks in Texas, this mountainous wilderness is especially rich in the fossils of animals that once lived in the sea. Humans have had a presence in the region for as long as 12,000 years—as witnessed by discoveries of ancient spear tips, baskets, and pottery.

Peregrine falcons catch prey, usually small birds, on the wing.

EL CAPITAN

This 8,085-ft- (2,464-m-) tall rock formation is made of ancient limestone pushed upward over millions of years. Exposed to wind and rain, it now reveals fossils of ancient fish, insects, and amphibians.

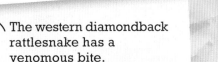

The western diamondback rattlesnake has a venomous bite.

FACTS

Size: 86,367 acres (349.51 km²)
Highest point: 8,749 ft (2,667 m) at Guadalupe Peak
Visitors each year: Almost 190,000

MCKITTRICK CANYON

This canyon is known for its colorful fall foliage, when tree leaves turn to bold shades of red, gold, and orange. Such scenes are rare in desert landscapes.

93

GREAT BASIN

NEVADA ESTABLISHED 1986

Great Basin National Park is part of the Great Basin region that covers much of the Western United States. It is a cold-desert environment where caves, forests, and mountains exist side by side. The world's longest-living tree—the bristlecone pine—grows in the park.

The oldest known **bristlecone pine** in the park lived to almost 5,000 years

WHEELER PEAK

The tallest mountain in the park is Wheeler Peak, which stands at 13,063 ft (3,982 m) and is part of the Snake Range. A grove of bristlecone pines grows on its northeastern side.

PARK HABITATS

- ⛰ Mountain
- 🌲 Coniferous forest
- 🏔 Cave
- 🌵 Desert

A diversity of habitats is found here, ranging from low desert to mountain tundra. The oldest living trees survive in forests high up in the mountains. Underground, there are four distinct groups of caves in the park.

Prince's plume can survive on little water.

STARRY NIGHT SKIES

Great Basin is called an International Dark Sky Park. On a clear night, stars, planets, meteors, and the Milky Way galaxy can be seen with the naked eye.

On summer nights, park rangers join guests on the "Star Train" to talk about the spectacular night sky.

LEHMAN CAVES

Visitors can take a tour of the park's caves, where they can marvel up close at stalactites, stalagmites, and other rare rock formations.

ARCHES

UTAH ESTABLISHED 1971

Arches National Park is home to the largest collection of arch formations in the world, with more than 2,000 on record. As well as these rocky bridges, the park contains potholes, balanced rocks, pinnacles, and domes that have been carved and shaped by water and weathering over thousands of years.

The park's **potholes** provide habitats for fairy shrimp, tadpole shrimp, and clam shrimp.

LANDSCAPE ARCH

This giant sandstone arch is 290 ft (88 m) wide. Landscape is the fifth-longest natural arch in the world and the longest in North America. Arches are the remains of rock that sat over domes of salt left by ancient seas that rain has dissolved over time.

MULE DEER

Mule deer, named for their mule-like ears, are common in the park. They feed on plants and are most active at dawn and dusk when temperatures are lower.

DESERT ANIMALS

During the baking heat of the day, many creatures in Arches hide from the sun. Apart from lizards and birds, animals can be hard to see. Many, such as the white-throated woodrat, are nocturnal, only coming out in the cooler nighttime.

 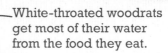
White-throated woodrats get most of their water from the food they eat.

The Utah juniper tree has scalelike leaves that help it retain water.

THE FACTS

Size: 76,679 acres (310.30 km²)
Highest point: 5,653 ft (1,723 m) at Elephant Butte
Visitors each year: About 1.7 million

Juniper berries are eaten by birds, coyotes, and other animals.

UTAH JUNIPER

This tree is native to the deserts of the western United States. It has deep roots that seek out any water, and can live for several hundred years.

THEODORE ROOSEVELT

NORTH DAKOTA

ESTABLISHED 1978

This protected landscape is filled with badlands, grasslands, and forests, and is home to herds of wild horses and bison. It honors President Theodore Roosevelt, who established five national parks during his presidency.

FACTS

Size: 70,447 acres (285.09 km²)
Highest point: 2,865 ft (873 m) at Peck Hill
Visitors each year: About 700,000

MALTESE CROSS RANCH CABIN

President Roosevelt bought the large Maltese Cross Cabin in 1883. Today, it is a historical landmark and contains some of his personal possessions, including his traveling trunk.

BISON

The park has two large herds of American bison, numbering several hundred. They are descended from 29 bison that were brought in from Nebraska in 1956.

The prairie rattlesnake lives in rocky outcrops and empty prairie dog tunnels, and hibernates during winter.

DRY TORTUGAS

FLORIDA ESTABLISHED 1992

About 70 miles (113 km) off the coast of southern Florida is a chain of seven main islands. Sea turtles and fish swim among precious coral reefs and shipwrecks in the turquoise waters surrounding them. "Tortugas" means "turtles" in Spanish.

About 80,000 sooty terns migrate to Bush Key in the park to nest each year.

FORT JEFFERSON

Fort Jefferson was built in the 19th century. The six-sided building is the third-largest fort in the United States. During the Civil War, it was used as a prison.

Scuba divers can explore shipwrecks, like the Windjammer, near Loggerhead Key.

SEA TURTLES

Five species of sea turtles, including the loggerhead, can be seen in the waters around the islands of Dry Tortugas.

FACTS

Size: 64,701 acres (261.84 km²)
Highest point: 10 ft (3 m) at Loggerhead Key
Visitors each year: Almost 80,000

99

WONDERS OF THE UNDERWORLD

This magical underworld includes many marvels—prehistoric drawings made by American Indians, colonies of bats, stalactites, stalagmites, and other rock formations. There are even rare fossils of up to 20 different species of sharks!

PARK HABITATS

 Cave

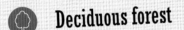 **Deciduous forest**

River

Grassland

Many animals have adapted to living in the dark caves and rely on senses other than vision. Aboveground, forests, waterways, and grasslands support much wildlife.

Many wildflowers, including fire pinks, grow in the park.

MAMMOTH CAVE

KENTUCKY ESTABLISHED 1941

A UNESCO World Heritage site, Mammoth Cave is the longest known cave system on Earth. It has more than 400 miles (644 km) of caverns. Inside its massive chambers, jaw-dropping rock formations are protected under huge limestone ceilings. Outside the cave are forest trails and rivers to explore.

Several species of bats, including the **Indiana bat**, live in Mammoth Cave.

THE FACTS

Size: 54,012 acres (218.58 km²)
Highest point: 925 ft (282 m)
at Mammoth Cave Ridge
Visitors each year: More than 550,000

TWO RIVERS

The Green and Nolin rivers run for 30 miles (48 km) through the overground area of the park. Boating provides a great way for visitors to enjoy the lush Kentucky landscape.

CAVE DWELLERS

Where there is water and moisture, there is life! Insects, worms, salamanders, cave shrimp, and cave crayfish (above), as well as bats, survive in the park's dark tunnels.

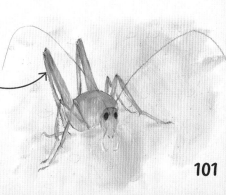

Cave crickets are flightless insects. Their long antennas help them find food and avoid predators.

MESA VERDE

COLORADO ESTABLISHED 1906

Mesa Verde is the only park created solely to protect the heritage of a people and their culture. More than 700 years ago, Ancestral Puebloans built villages beneath steep sandstone cliffs, high above the Montezuma Valley. About 600 of their cliff dwellings survive today.

FACTS

Size: 52,485 acres (212.40 km²)

Highest point: 8,572 ft (2,613 m) at Park Point

Visitors each year: More than 550,000

CLIFF DWELLINGS

The dwellings are made from sticks and sandstone. They vary from small, one-room huts to the multistory Cliff Palace, which could house about 100 people.

The caterpillars of many butterfly species, including the **black swallowtail**, live in the park.

CHAPIN MESA ARCHAEOLOGICAL MUSEUM

The park's museum was built in the 1920s from the same sandstone as the cliff dwellings. It displays prehistoric objects and dioramas of Ancestral Puebloan life.

The Ancient Puebloans created a style of pottery known as black-on-white.

102

ACADIA

MAINE ESTABLISHED 1919

One of the most visited national parks, Acadia is treasured for its beautiful forests, mountains, lakes, streams, and beaches. The park lies off the coast of Maine and covers about half of Mount Desert Island and several nearby, small islands.

FACTS

Size: 49,077 acres (198.6 km²)
Highest point: 1,530 ft (466 m) at Cadillac Mountain
Visitors each year: More than 3.4 million

Jordan Pond House has been serving tea and popovers since the 1890s.

JORDAN POND

This mountain lake was formed by a glacier. Its waters are crystal clear, and it reaches a depth of more than 150 ft (46 m).

Native bees are "super-pollinators" and vital for the survival of many native plants.

The wood lily's colorful petals attract bumblebees and other pollinators.

CADILLAC MOUNTAIN

The peak of Cadillac Mountain has great views out across the wild Atlantic coast. In winter, this part of the United States is the first to get the sun's morning rays.

CARLSBAD CAVERNS

NEW MEXICO ESTABLISHED 1930

Beneath the surface of the Guadalupe Mountains on the Texas–New Mexico state line is Carlsbad Caverns—a system of more than 100 limestone cave chambers, with many awe-inspiring rock formations. Aboveground, there is a desert landscape.

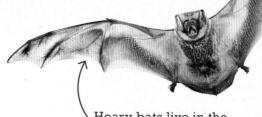

Hoary bats live in the park. Their main source of food is moths.

THE BIG ROOM

The largest cave chamber in Carlsbad Caverns is known as the Big Room. It's the fifth-largest cave chamber in North America. It contains some of the best-known features of the park, such as the Bottomless Pit.

Javelinas move through the shrubs above Carlsbad Caverns. These animals look similar to pigs but are a different species.

PARK HABITATS

Mountain

Desert

Cave

The caves are a habitat for bats and other creatures. Outside the caves, many plants and animals have adapted to live in the harsh, dry conditions of the hot desert and rugged mountains.

More than **350 bird species**, including the ladder-backed woodpecker, have been seen in the park.

LECHUGUILLA CAVE

Expert cave explorers have mapped out more than 145 miles (233 km) of this lengthy limestone cave since 1984. It contains gypsum formations known as "chandeliers."

Cones are made by conifers such as the ponderosa pine, which grows in the park.

FACTS

Size: 46,766 acres (189.26 km²)
Highest point: 6,535 ft (1,992 m) at Guadalupe Ridge
Visitors each year: About 440,000

SHASTA GROUND SLOTH

The bones of a bear-sized ground sloth that lived about 11,000 years ago were found at a depth of 400 ft (122 m) in Carlsbad Caverns. The plant-eater probably fell into the cave.

STALACTITES AND STALAGMITES

The Carlsbad Caverns are full of stalactites and stalagmites, which are made from calcium carbonate and other minerals. Stalactites hang down from the ceiling, whereas stalagmites build up from the cave floor. If these two natural features grow long enough to fuse, the result is known as a column.

BRYCE CANYON

UTAH ESTABLISHED 1928

Bryce Canyon is not a single canyon at all, but it contains many valleys filled with spires of rock called hoodoos. The largest of these rocky mazes, Bryce Amphitheater, is 12 miles (19 km) long. The striped limestone of the park's rock formations attracts millions of visitors a year.

SCULPTED BY WATER

Mostly above 8,000 ft (2,438 m), the park regularly experiences freezing temperatures. When rain that has seeped into the rocks freezes, it expands. As the ice grows, it breaks the rock apart. Rain also dissolves some of the rock, shaping the hoodoos as in Bryce Amphitheater (below).

The **Great Basin rattlesnake** can "see" heat using special sensors.

THOR'S HAMMER

This hoodoo is named for its likeness to the hammer of Thor, the legendary Norse god of thunder.

Adult northern goshawks have gray feathers.

THE FACTS

Size: 35,835 acres (145.02 km²)
Highest point: 9,105 ft (2,775 m) at Rainbow Point
Visitors each year: About 2.6 million

NORTHERN GOSHAWK

These hawks perch on tree branches to watch for prey to eat. They can quickly swoop to catch their meal, usually smaller birds, squirrels, or rabbits.

The Bryce Canyon paintbrush is a rare flowering plant native to Utah.

PARK HABITATS

🌲 **Coniferous forest**

🔺 **Mountain**

〰 **River**

This park sits high up, where the fascinating rock formations are enclosed by a vast forest, which in turn is surrounded by desert. Wildlife thrives in all areas of the park.

Utah prairie dogs live in communities called "towns."

UTAH PRAIRIE DOG

These small mammals were reintroduced into the park after almost going extinct. Prairie dogs give alarm calls to warn each other if a predator, such as a hawk or coyote, has been spotted.

THE FACTS

Size: 33,971 acres (137.48 km²)
Highest point: 5,013 ft (1,528 m) at Rankin Ridge
Visitors each year: More than 615,000

WIND CAVE

SOUTH DAKOTA ESTABLISHED 1903

Wind Cave is one of the longest caves in the world—about 150 miles (241 km) of its rocky corridors have been explored. American Indians thought the whistling wind at the cave's entrance was breath from the underworld. Overground, bison, mule deer, pronghorn, elk, and coyotes roam the grassland.

BOXWORK

Wind Cave's ceilings are covered in boxwork rock formations. Made from tiny blades of rock that intersect in honeycomb patterns, these intriguing shapes are the largest and finest collection of their kind anywhere in the world!

The American kestrel preys on small prairie animals.

RED VALLEY

Here, deep-red and maroon cliffs made of mudstone, shale, and siltstone stand out in a serene meadow. Many animals pass through the valley to graze or hunt for food.

'Ākohekohe

HALEAKALĀ

HAWAI'I ESTABLISHED 1961

Located on the island of Maui, Haleakalā National Park stretches from the top of a giant volcano, which dominates the island's landscape, down to the coast. Home to precious forest birds and unusual plants, the park has trails for hikers, and cyclists can enjoy the breathtaking experience of riding down the volcano's side.

NATIVE FOREST BIRDS

A high forested area of the park, called the Important Bird Area, is home to rare species, such as the 'ākohekohe, 'i'iwi, and kiwikiu. These birds live nowhere else in the world.

Silverswords grow in the hot, dry, high slopes of the volcano.

Silverswords take decades to bloom and can live for as long as 90 years.

Silver geraniums reflect sunlight to stay cool.

THE FACTS

Size: 33,265 acres (134.62 km²)
Highest point: 10,023 ft (3,055 m) at Haleakalā Volcano
Visitors each year: Almost 1 million

HALEAKALĀ VOLCANO

A shield volcano—made of layer upon layer of dried lava flows—Haleakalā has 14 cinder cones in its summit valley. The volcano is dormant and last erupted 400 to 600 years ago. Its name means "house of the sun" in the Hawaiian language.

CUYAHOGA VALLEY

OHIO ESTABLISHED 2000

Cuyahoga Valley National Park is the only national park in Ohio. Its forests, rocky outcrops, wetlands, and waterfalls surround the meandering Cuyahoga River. Alongside its wealth of plants and wildlife, the park has many historic sites, including the oldest train still running in North America.

The great blue heron has a wingspan of up to 6.6 ft (2 m).

BEAVER MARSH

This marsh has an elevated boardwalk, from which visitors can watch wildlife. They might see beavers, muskrats, frogs, turtles, birds, and other creatures that live in these wetlands.

SCENIC RAILROAD

One of the park's biggest attractions is the historic Cuyahoga Valley Scenic Railroad. Along the nearly 150-year-old tracks, Locomotive No. 765 chugs through the park's gorgeous scenery.

PARK HABITATS

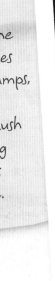

- **Deciduous forest**
- **Wetland**
- **River**

This park is centered around the Cuyahoga River, which branches off into wetlands, marshes, swamps, and streams. The landscape is rugged high above the river. Lush upland forests cover the rolling landscape. All these habitats support a diversity of wildlife.

Cuyahoga Valley has biking trails for cyclists.

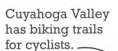

BRANDYWINE FALLS

Cascading 65 ft (20 m), Brandywine Falls is the tallest and most recognizable waterfall in the park. It has served as a landmark in the area for hundreds of years. Nearby pools attract salamanders.

Adult spotted salamanders spend most of their lives under logs or rocks, or in burrows made by other animals.

THE FACTS

Size: 32,572 acres (131.81 km²)
Highest point: 1,164 ft (355 m) at Brush Road
Visitors each year: More than 2.2 million

BLACK CANYON OF THE GUNNISON

COLORADO ESTABLISHED 1999

At its deepest point, the Black Canyon reaches a dizzying depth of 2,722 ft (830 m)—truly an impressive sight. The park surrounds the Gunnison River, which cuts through the sheer cliffs, crashing over rocks and rapids, before feeding into the Colorado River downstream.

The park was named for the dark shadows on the walls of the canyon.

GUNNISON RIVER

About two million years ago, the Gunnison River began to flow. Over time, it carved its way through the rock to form the huge 48-mile (77-km) Black Canyon.

GREAT HORNED OWL

These owls love to hunt the rabbits and rodents that scrabble around the canyon rims at night. Their round, dish-like faces direct sounds toward their ears, so they can hear even the tiniest of movements in the dark.

Gambel oak leaves are a favorite food of the mule deer in the park.

THE FACTS

Size: 30,780 acres (124.56 km²)
Highest point: 9,040 ft (2,755 m) at Poison Spring Hill
Visitors each year: More than 430,000

PINNACLES

The bright **yellow** bush poppy thrives in the rocky soil at Pinnacles.

CALIFORNIA ESTABLISHED 2013

This park is part of the remains of an ancient volcano that was formed more than 23 million years ago. The volcano was split by the movement of Earth's plates. Since then, Pinnacles has moved north by 195 miles (314 km) to its current location—and it continues to move by 1 in (2.5 cm) each year.

THE FACTS

Size: 26,686 acres (107.99 km²)
Highest point: 3,304 ft (1,007 m)
at North Chalone Peak
Visitors each year:
Almost 180,000

CAVES AND BATS

There are caves in the park that are home to several species of bats, including Townsend's big-eared bat. These caves formed when giant boulders fell into narrow ravines, creating rocky roofs.

SPIRES OF ROCK

Pinnacles is named for the distinctive spires of rock in the park. They are made of volcanic rock and, over millions of years, have been sculpted by the wind and rain into the tall towers we see today.

Townsend's big-eared bats usually live about 16 years.

CONGAREE

SOUTH CAROLINA ESTABLISHED 2003

Congaree is known for its low-lying, old forest, which includes some of the tallest trees in the Eastern United States—and its rich diversity of wildlife. The park is located in a river floodplain. Flooding happens about 10 times a year, and the waters bring valuable nutrients to the forests.

Poison ivy vines

THE FACTS

Size: 26,476 acres (107.14 km^2)
Highest point: 140 ft (43 m) at Old Buff Road
Visitors each year: Almost 160,000

RIVER OTTERS

North American river otters live in the park. They hunt in the rivers, lakes, and marshes. Their favorite food is fish, but they also eat turtles, frogs, salamanders, and crayfish.

Bald cypress tree trunks can measure up to 26 ft (8 m) around their base.

CEDAR CREEK

The main waterway flowing through Congaree is Cedar Creek. Paddling and fishing are two popular ways to enjoy the creek, which stretches for 15 miles (24 km) through hardwood forest.

INDIANA DUNES

INDIANA ESTABLISHED 2019

This park is named for its sand dunes that started to form more than 13,000 years ago during the last ice age. It is home to bogs, marshes, forests, streams, and prairies all beside the vast waters of Lake Michigan. Wildflowers, birds, and mammals thrive in this varied national park.

The Chellberg Farmhouse was built in 1885. It was the home of a family from Sweden.

THE FACTS

Size: 15,349 acres (62.12 km²)
Highest point: 902 ft (275 m) at High Point
Visitors each year: More than 2.1 million

Red admiral butterflies flutter in the wetlands during spring.

A FIT FOR ALL SEASONS

Each season offers its own magic at Indiana Dunes. Wildflowers line the trails during spring. Sunsets make summer a favorite time of year. Fall's colorful leaves blanket the landscape. Winter is a great time for snowshoeing across snowy paths.

FUN AT THE BEACH

The park has 15 miles (24 km) of shoreline, at the southern tip of Lake Michigan. Visitors can enjoy beach activities, such as swimming. West Beach is the most popular beach.

117

VIRGIN ISLANDS

VIRGIN ISLANDS ESTABLISHED 1956

US Virgin Islands National Park is made up of beautiful beaches, tropical forests, and sloping mountains. Protected parkland extends into the sea off the island of St. John, where sea turtles, stingrays, and sharks swim through coral reefs. Ruins of sugar plantations dot the landscape, hinting at the park's history.

THE FACTS

Size: 15,052 acres (60.91 km^2)
Highest point: 1,286 ft (392 m) at Bordeaux Mountain
Visitors each year: More than 130,000

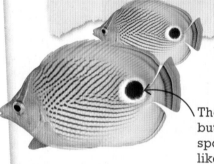

The foureye butterflyfish has spots that look like big eyes.

YAWZI POINT TRAIL

The Yawzi Point Trail follows a short, 0.3-mile (0.5-km) path among the ruins of plantations. The trail ends at Yawzi Point, overlooking the coastlines of two bays.

WHITE SAND BEACHES

This park is known for its powdery white sand beaches that stretch into crystal-clear waters where fish and sea turtles swim among the corals. Trunk Bay is the most popular beach, with an underwater snorkeling trail that points out features of interest.

AMERICAN SAMOA

AMERICAN SAMOA ESTABLISHED 1988

Located in the South Pacific, the National Park of American Samoa is the only national park south of the equator. Its protected areas are spread across three islands—Ta'ū, Ofu, and Tutuila. Fruit bats, coral reefs, and tropical rainforests can be found here, as well as the 3,000-year-old Samoan culture.

THE FACTS

Size: 8,257 acres (33.41 km²)
Highest point: 3,159 ft (963 m)
at Lata Mountain
Visitors each year:
About 60,000

↑ The Samoan fruit bat is one of three native bat species in American Samoa.

THE SAMOAN PEOPLE

The Samoan culture is one of the oldest in Polynesia. Communities are made up of extended families, who keep their traditions alive.

CORAL REEFS

There are more than 250 species of corals in the park, and they serve as nurseries for tropical fish, sharks, and other aquatic life. The 350-acre (1.42-km²) reef at Ofu Beach is easily seen through the clear waters and is the most visited site in the park.

HOT SPRINGS

ARKANSAS ESTABLISHED 1921

Water heated deep underground flows from 47 springs in this historic national park. The surrounding Ouachita Mountains have more than 20 miles (32 km) of trails, where explorers will find both American Indian artifacts and rich wildlife.

Male northern cardinals have bright-red plumage.

THE FACTS

Size: 5,554 acres (22.48 km²)
Highest point: 1,405 ft (428 m) at Music Mountain
Visitors each year: Almost 1.5 million

Eight historic spas line the famous Bathhouse Row.

THE AMERICAN SPA

American Indians have been visiting the springs for centuries and named the area the "Valley of the Vapors." In the 1800s, a spa town was built around the springs, and it began welcoming guests to the soothing properties of the waters.

NINE-BANDED ARMADILLO

This well-armored mammal is named for the bands of scales on its hard shell. It is mostly active at night, lives on its own, and feeds on insects.

GATEWAY ARCH

MISSOURI ESTABLISHED 2018

Gateway Arch is the tallest monument in any of the national parks. It is known as the "Gateway to the West." It symbolizes President Thomas Jefferson's push into the western United States, following the Louisiana Purchase, and the expedition of Meriwether Lewis and William Clark.

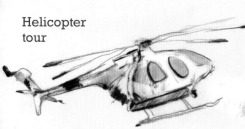

Riverboat cruises offer visitors clear views of the arch.

GATEWAY ARCH

Made from stainless steel, the Gateway Arch is 630 ft (192 m) tall. It was opened to the public in 1967. There is an observation deck at the top, which people can reach by tram.

Helicopter tour

OLD COURTHOUSE

This 19th-century courthouse used to have 12 courtrooms. It now has only two—one is preserved to look as it did in the 1850s, and the other as it did in the 1910s.

THE FACTS

Size: 193 acres (0.78 km²)
Highest point: 630 ft (192 m) above ground level at the top of the arch
Visitors each year: About 2 million

WILDLIFE SPOTTING

National parks are great places to see wild animals in their natural environment. Across the United States, hundreds of different kinds of animals make their homes in the parks, from huge bison and moose to beautiful butterflies and tiny beetles.

TOP TIPS

Here are some handy tips to help you spot animals when visiting a national park.

Ask a park ranger—he or she will be able to tell you the best places to see animals that live in the park.

Take binoculars if you have a pair or can borrow some. They're great for seeing faraway animals up close.

Look above you—there may be birds, bats, or butterflies flying over you or a raccoon watching you from in a tree.

If you think you see a movement, stand still and watch. You may make out a lizard blending in against a rock or a jackrabbit whose coat matches the soil.

Red admiral

Don't be noisy— that's a sure way to scare off animals.

Do some research before you go to a park. Check the park's website to see which animals live there or which ones, such as migrating birds, might be passing through.

Look for splashes of color. Some animals, especially birds, are brightly colored. That makes them easy to spot in the trees or on the ground when looking for food.

⚠ Warning

Do not approach, chase, or feed wild animals. It is their home—not yours— so please respect that at all times. Before your visit, make sure you check the park's website for its guidelines on staying safe when watching wildlife.

Northern cardinal

Grizzly bear

Greater roadrunner

Front paws are smaller than the back ones.

Two toes face forward and two back.

ANIMAL TRACKS

Many animals keep themselves hidden away. There may be signs, though, that they are around, such as their tracks. If you find tracks in wet soil or sand, or snow, take a photo to help you identify them later.

The split hooves are heart-shaped.

Fishers' feet have five toes.

Fisher

Mule deer

LOOKING OUT FOR SCAT

Another sign that animals are in the area is their poop, which is called scat. If you find some scat, make sure you don't touch it—it will contain germs. Take a photo and ask a park ranger to identify which animal left it.

Mountain lion and its scat (left)

GLOSSARY

alpine High up in the mountains

archaeologist Someone who studies people and societies from the past through their remains, such as pottery, walls, and jewelry

badland Rocky area with poor soil, few plants, and often unusual rock formations

camouflage Colors or patterns that help an animal blend in with its surroundings

canopy Layer in a forest made up of the leafy crowns of most of the trees

canyon Long, deep, narrow valley between two cliffs, usually with a river flowing through it

capitol Government building in which lawmakers meet

cinder cone Cone-shaped hill of volcanic-rock fragments around a volcanic opening

climate change Process of Earth's weather patterns changing over time due to natural causes or human activity

coniferous Word used to refer to cone-bearing trees and shrubs, such as pines and firs

conservation Protecting environments and plant and animal life

crater Bowl-shaped hollow in the ground, often formed by the collapse of a volcano after it has erupted

deciduous Word used to refer to trees and shrubs that shed their leaves in fall

diorama Museum exhibit showing a natural or historic scene with models of figures in front of a backdrop

dormant Word used to describe a volcano during an inactive stage or an animal in a deep sleep-like state that lets it survive through a harsh period, such as winter

drought Period of very low or no rainfall

dune Mound of sand blown into its shape by the wind

environment Surroundings in which an animal, plant, or other life-form lives

estuary Mouth of a large river where it joins the sea, and fresh and salt water mix

extinction When a species dies out completely

food chain Series of feeding links by which energy passes from one organism to another: for example, a plant is eaten by a prairie dog, which is in turn eaten by a bird of prey

geothermal Word used to describe heat produced naturally underground

geyser Hot spring that spurts a column of water and steam into the air

glacier Large body of ice and rock that moves slowly down a slope

glacier calving Breaking off of huge chunks of ice at the front of a glacier that has reached the sea or a lake. These chunks become icebergs

gorge Another word for a canyon

granite Very hard, grainy volcanic rock

gypsum Soft, crystalline mineral, often see-through or white

habitat Natural home or environment of a species

hardwood Strong, hard wood from non-coniferous trees, such as oak and ash

hibernation Spending winter in a deep sleep-like state to avoid harsh conditions or a shortage of food

hot spring Spring from which flows hot water that is heated naturally underground

ice age Period in Earth's history when it was much colder

icefield Vast area of thick ice, usually in a polar region

invasive Plant or animal that rapidly increases in numbers in a particular area, often causing harm

lava tube Tunnel through volcanic rock that was made by flowing lava

light pollution Brightening of the night sky due to human-made light sources, such as street lights, especially in cities

Louisiana Purchase Buying of land from France by President Thomas Jefferson, in 1803, that doubled the size of the United States

Lower 48 states All of the US states except Alaska and Hawai'i

mangrove Tree or shrub that grows on coasts and riverbanks—with some of its roots aboveground—that can withstand salt water; a forest of such plants

microbe Tiny living thing, such as a bacterium or protozoan; also called a microorganism

migration Seasonal movement of animals from one place to another to breed, find food, or escape harsh weather

mud pot Pool of hot, bubbling mud found in geothermal areas, such as near volcanoes

mural Painting or etching made on a wall

native Word used to describe species that originate or are found naturally in an area

naturalist Someone who studies animals, plants, and other living things

Northern Lights Colorful light displays in the sky in Arctic regions; also called Aurora Borealis

petrified Turned into stone

pigment Natural substance that gives an animal or plant its color

plantation Large estate that grows a crop such as sugar, coffee, or rubber

plateau Area of high, mostly flat ground

pollinate Transfer tiny grains from flower to flower so that seeds can be made

Polynesia Area of the Pacific Ocean with more than one thousand islands, including Hawai'i, American Samoa, and New Zealand

popover Light, hollow cake made from a thin batter

pothole Hole in the ground, often filled with water

preserve Protected area that often allows traditional hunting and resource mining

ravine Narrow valley with steep sides, usually smaller than a canyon

reef Long bar of rocks, sand, or coral just below the surface of water

salt flat Flat area covered in a crusty layer of salt left when a pool of water dried up

snowshoe Large, flat attachment to footwear that stops the wearer sinking into snow

spawning When certain animals, such as fish or frogs, lay their eggs in water

species Group of similar plants, animals, or other life-forms that share characteristics different from other groups

stalactite Piece of rock that hangs down from the roof of a cave and looks like an icicle

stalagmite Pointed piece of rock slowly growing upward from the floor of a cave

steam vent Opening in the ground through which steam and volcanic gases are released

tectonic plate Large, slow-moving piece of the Earth's crust and upper mantle

temperate Word used to describe regions of the world with mild temperatures and distinct seasons

tepee Cone-shaped tent of animal hides or canvas around a frame of poles that can be put up and taken down quickly; traditionally used by American Indians

thermophile Bacterium or another microbe that survives best under very hot conditions

tundra Treeless region, often frozen for much of the year, covered by low-growing plants

venomous Word used to describe animals that inject a poisonous substance, called a venom, when they bite or sting

vulnerable Word used to describe a species or population at high risk of extinction unless changes are made to protect it

wetland Wet, muddy land, such as a swamp, marsh, or bog, often covered in wild plants

wilderness Area of wild land undisturbed by humans

INDEX

ACKNOWLEDGMENTS

The publisher would like to thank the following people for their assistance in the preparation of this book: Seeta Parmar and Graeme Williams for editorial assistance; Megan Douglass and Caroline Stamps for proofreading; and Helen Peters for compiling the index.

The publisher would like to thank the following for their kind permission to reproduce their photographs:

(Key: a-above; b-below/bottom; c-center; f-far; l-left; r-right; t-top)

2 Dreamstime.com: Dana Kenneth Johnson (bl). **2–3 Dreamstime.com:** Chaoss (Background). **4 Alamy Stock Photo:** Johner Images (c). **Dreamstime.com:** Galyna Andrushko (cra). **5 123RF.com:** picsfive (cl). **Alamy Stock Photo:** Norma Jean Gargasz (tr). **Dreamstime.com:** Robert Philip (bl). **8 123RF.com:** stillfx (tr). **8–9 Alamy Stock Photo:** UDAZKENA (c). **Dreamstime.com:** Daboost (Notebook); Emir Hodzic. **9 123RF.com:** picsfive (bl). **Dreamstime.com:** Davidhoffmannphotography (tl); Jaanall (cr). **Getty Images:** TCYuen (tr). **10–11 Dreamstime.com:** Joe Sohm. **10 Dreamstime.com:** Yellowdesignstudio (clb). **12 123RF.com:** picsfive (tr). **12–13 Alamy Stock Photo:** Design Pics Inc / Alaska Stock / Patrick Endres (clb). **Dreamstime.com:** Daboost (Notebook). **13 123RF.com:** picsfive (bl). **Alamy Stock Photo:** LOETSCHER CHLAUS (tl). **Dreamstime.com:** Sergei Kozminov (ca, br). **14 123RF.com:** stillfx (bl). **Dreamstime.com:** Jonathan Mauer (tr). **14–15 Alamy Stock Photo:** NPS Photo (cb). **Dreamstime.com:** Daboost (Notebook); Viacheslav Voloshyn. **15 Alamy Stock Photo:** Accent Alaska.com (cr); Skip Moody / Dembinsky Photo Associates (cl). **16–17 Dreamstime.com:** Daboost (Notebook); Christian De Grandmaison. **16 123RF.com:** stillfx (cra). **Getty Images:** Gallo Images / Danita Delimont (cb). **17 123RF.com:** picsfive (cr). **Alamy Stock Photo:** All Canada Photos / Roberta Olenick (cl); National Geographic Image Collection / Ralph Lee Hopkins (tr). **Dreamstime.com:** Tony Campbell (bl). **iStockphoto.com:** JHVEPhoto (br). **18 123RF.com:** stillfx (bl). **Dreamstime.com:** Moose Henderson (tr). **18–19 Alamy Stock Photo:** Design Pics Inc / Mike Criss (cb). **Dreamstime.com:** Daboost (Notebook); Beatriz Navarro. **19 123RF.com:** picsfive (tl). **Alamy Stock Photo:** Natural History Library (tr); Natural History Library (ca). **Dreamstime.com:** Steven Prorak (br). **20 123RF.com:** stillfx (br). **Alamy Stock Photo:** Doug Horrigan (tr). **Dreamstime.com:** Biolifepics (crb, bc). **20–21 Dreamstime.com:** Daboost (Notebook); Emir Hodzic (Background). **21 123RF.com:** picsfive (tr). **Dreamstime.com:** Biolifepics (cl). **Getty Images:** Carol Polich Photo Workshops (cla). **Unsplash:** Tanya Nevidoma (br). **22 iStockphoto.com:** sorincolac (bl). **22–23 Dreamstime.com:** Daboost (Notebook); Liliya Kandrashevich. **23 123RF.com:** picsfive (cr). **Alamy Stock Photo:** Agefotostock / Pixtal (cla); National Geographic Image Collection / JONATHAN IRISH (tr); Scenics & Science (cb). **Dreamstime.com:** Jnjhuz (crb). **24–25 Dreamstime.com:** Bennymarty. **24 123RF.com:** picsfive (bl). **26 123RF.com:** MJ - tim Fotografie (ca); picsfive (bl). **Alamy Stock Photo:** Spring Images (br). **26–27 Dreamstime.com:** Daboost (Notebook); Luckyphotographer (c); Viacheslav Voloshyn. **27 123RF.com:** stillfx (cr). **Alamy Stock Photo:** imageBROKER / Horst Mahr (tr). **Dreamstime.com:** Birdiegal717 (b). **28 123RF.com:** picsfive (br). **Courtesy of National Park Service, Lewis and Clark National Historic Trail:** NPS Photo / Emily Mesner (clb). **28–29 Alamy Stock Photo:** SuperStock / RGB Ventures / Fred & Randi Hirschmann (c). **Dreamstime.com:** Daboost (Notebook). **29 123RF.com**: picsfive (c). **Alamy Stock Photo:** Design Pics Inc / Nick Jans (bl). **Dreamstime.com:** Robynmac / Robyn Mackenzie (cr). **Courtesy of National Park Service, Lewis and Clark National Historic Trail:** NPS Photo (tr). **30–31 Dreamstime.com:** Daboost (Notebook); Radekgibran. **30 123RF.com:** picsfive (cra). **Dreamstime.com:** Bonnie Fink (c). **Getty Images:** Tetra Images (cb). **31 123RF.com:** picsfive (cl). **Alamy Stock Photo:** Rick & Nora Bowers (cr). **Dreamstime.com:** Sandi Cullifer (bc); Dpselvaggi (bl). **32 123RF.com:** picsfive (br). **Alamy Stock Photo:** Nature Picture Library / naturepl.com / Claudio Contreras Koob (cb). **Dreamstime.com:** Kojihirano (bl). **32–33 Alamy Stock Photo:** Radek Hofman (c). **Dreamstime.com:** Daboost. **33 123RF.com:** picsfive (cra). **Dreamstime.com:** Florence Mcginn (br). **34 123RF.com:** picsfive (tl). **34–35 Dreamstime.com:** Oksanaphoto. **36 123RF.com:** picsfive (cl). **Dreamstime.com:** Maksershov (cr); Paulstansbury73 (tc). **36–37 Dreamstime.com:** Daboost (Notebook). **37 123RF.com:** picsfive (tr). **Dreamstime.com:** Jenifoto406 (cr); William Perry (clb); Yellowdesignstudio (ca). **38–39 Dreamstime.com:** Daboost (Notebook). **iStockphoto.com:** Pgiam. **38 123RF.com:** Pancaketom / Tom Grundy (bc). **Dreamstime.com:** Bolotov (br); Larry Gevert (cr). **Getty Images:** Moment / J. LINDHARDT Photography (tr). **39 123RF.com:** picsfive (tr). **Dreamstime.com:** Byelikova (bl). **40 123RF.com:** picsfive (tr). **Alamy Stock Photo:** Inge Johnsson (br). **Dreamstime.com:** Hakoar (bl). **40–41 Dreamstime.com:** Daboost (Notebook); Beatriz Navarro. **41 123RF.com:** picsfive (bl). **Alamy Stock Photo:** Janice and Nolan Braud (cr). **Dreamstime.com:** Ztiger (tl). **iStockphoto.com:** E+ / lucentius (tr). **42 123RF.com:** Natalie Ruffing (b). **Dreamstime.com:** Bolotov (cl). **42–43 123RF.com:** Aleksandr Frolov (background). **Dreamstime.com:** Daboost. **43 123RF.com:** picsfive (crb). **Dreamstime.com:** Maria Luisa Lopez Estivill (tr); Brian Lasenby (clb). **Getty Images:** Photodisc / R. Andrew Odum (cla). **44 Alamy Stock Photo:** Grantmulli / Stockimo (c). **Dreamstime.com:** Robynmac / Robyn Mackenzie (br). **44–45 Alamy Stock Photo:** Stefano Politi Markovina (c). **Dreamstime.com:** Daboost (Noteboo); Natalia Shabasheva. **45 123RF.com:** picsfive (tr). **Dreamstime.com:** Jeffrey Banke (cra); Sorin Colac (br). **46 123RF.com:** stillfx (br). **Alamy Stock Photo:** Michelle Holihan (cr); Michelle Holihan (bl). **46–47 Dreamstime.com:** Daboost (notebook); Liliya Kandrashevich. **47 123RF.com:** picsfive (br). **Alamy Stock Photo:** M. Timothy O'Keefe (ca). **48 Alamy Stock Photo:** Nature Picture Library / Floris van Breugel (tr). **Dreamstime.com:** Sean Pavone (clb); Sean Pavone (b). **48–49 Dreamstime.com:** Daboost (Notebook); Christian De Grandmaison. **49 123RF.com:** picsfive (tl); stillfx (crb). **Dreamstime.com:** Sgoodwin4813 (bc); Starryvoyage (clb). **50–51 Dreamstime.com:** Daveallenphoto. **51 123RF.com:** picsfive (br). **52 123RF.com:** stillfx (br). **Dreamstime.com:** Gatito33 (cra); Lore Patterson (c). **52–53 123RF.com:** Marina Scurupii. **Dreamstime.com:** Cheriecokeley (b); Daboost (Notebook). **53 Dreamstime.com:** Robynmac / Robyn Mackenzie (tr). **Getty Images:** Tacoma News Tribune / Drew Perine (cla). **54 Alamy Stock Photo:** Russ Bishop (cl); Leon Werdinger (bl). **54–55 Dreamstime.com:** Daboost (Notebook); Colin Young (tc); Ross Henry. **55 123RF.com:** picsfive (bl); stillfx (tr). **Alamy Stock Photo:** Brian Jannsen (cra). **Dreamstime.com:** Colin Young (crb); Yellowdesignstudio (cr). **56 123RF.com:** picsfive (br). **Alamy Stock Photo:** Jim West (cl). **Dreamstime.com:** Will Reece (bc). **56–57 Dreamstime.com:** Daboost. **Getty Images:** Perspectives / Joe Carini (c). **57 123RF.com:** picsfive (tc). **Dreamstime.com:** Annegordon (fcr); Bolotov (cr). **Getty Images:** U.S. Geological Survey (tr). **iStockphoto.com:** Westend61 (bl). **58–59 Dreamstime.com:** Shane Myers. **58 123RF.com:** picsfive (tl). **Dreamstime.com:** Chih-cheng Chang (cla). **60–61 Dreamstime.com:** Daboost. **Getty Images:** The Image Bank Unreleased / Galen Rowell (tc). **60 123RF.com:** stillfx (br). **iStockphoto.com:** E+ / Bobbushphoto (cb). **61 123RF.com:** picsfive (clb). **62 123RF.com:** stillfx (br). **Alamy Stock Photo:** Sean Xu (bl). **Dorling Kindersley:** (cra). **Dreamstime.com:** Tupungato (clb). **62–63 Dreamstime.com:** Daboost (Notebook); Pimonpim Tangosol. **63 123RF.com:** picsfive (cr). **Alamy Stock Photo:** Toroverde (tl). **64–65 Dreamstime.com:** Brenda Denmark. **64 123RF.com:** picsfive (bl). **66–67 Dreamstime.com:** Daboost (Notebook); Pimonpim Tangosol. **66 123RF.com:** picsfive (cra). **Alamy Stock Photo:** George H.H. Huey (br). **67 123RF.com:** picsfive (cr). **Alamy Stock Photo:** Blue Planet Archive DFL (cla); WaterFrame_jdo (tr). **68–69 Dreamstime.com:** Daboost (Notebook); Tirachard Kumtanom. **68 Dreamstime.com:** Gary Gray (bl); Phillip Lowe (cra); Kerry Hargrove (tr). **69 123RF.com:** picsfive (cl). **Alamy Stock Photo:** Niebrugge Images (bc). **Dreamstime.com:** Edmund Lowe (cra). **iStockphoto.com:** Natalie Ruffing (crb). **70 Dreamstime.com:** Mirror Images (tr). **iStockphoto.com:** Creative Edge (cr). **70–71 Dreamstime.com:** Daboost (Notebook). **71 123RF.com:** picsfive (tr); stillfx (bl). **Dreamstime.com:** F11photo (br); Brian Kushner (tl). **72 123RF.com:** picsfive (cra). **Alamy Stock Photo:** Norman Wharton (b). **72–73 Dreamstime.com:** Daboost (Notebook); Christian De Grandmaison. **73 123RF.com:** stillfx (tr). **Dreamstime.com:** Rinus Baak (bl, br); Photowitch (crb); David Hayes (tl). **74 123RF.com:** picsfive (tr). **Alamy Stock Photo:** Don Breneman (crb). **iStockphoto.com:** rpbirdman (bl). **74–75 Dreamstime.com:** Daboost (Notebook); Viacheslav Voloshyn. **75 123RF.com:** picsfive (cl). **Alamy Stock Photo:** Rebecca Brown (bl). **Dreamstime.com:** Jon Bilous (tr); Psnaturephotography (cb). **76–77 Dreamstime.com:** Daboost (Notebook); Vinesh Kumar. **76 123RF.com:** stillfx (bl). **Alamy Stock Photo:** Curved Light USA (tr). **Dreamstime.com:** Aiisha (crb). **77 123RF.com:** picsfive (cr). **Dreamstime.com:** Kwiktor (tr). **National Park Service:** (br). **78–79 Dreamstime.com:** Hotshotsworldwide. **78 123RF.com:** picsfive (tl). **80–81 Dreamstime.com:** Chernetskaya; Daboost (Notebook). **80 123RF.com:** picsfive (tr). **Alamy Stock Photo:** Stephen Frink Collection / Stephen Frink (crb). **81 123RF.com:** picsfive (bl). **Alamy Stock Photo:** Bob Gibbons (tr). **Dreamstime.com:** Francisco Blanco (cra). **iStockphoto.com:** ArendTrent (br). **82–83 Dreamstime.com:** Daboost (Notebook). **Getty Images:** 500px Prime / Mila Hofman (bc). **82 Dreamstime.com:** Robynmac / Robyn Mackenzie (tr); Twildlife (cra). **83 123RF.com:** picsfive (cb). **Alamy Stock Photo:** Natural History Archive (tr). **Dreamstime.com:** Pancaketom (br). **iStockphoto.com:** milehightraveler (cla). **84 123RF.com:** picsfive (tl). **84–85 Getty Images:** EyeEm / Michael Scace. **86 123RF.com:** picsfive (tr). **Alamy Stock Photo:** Michele Falzone (cb). **86–87 Dreamstime.com:** Daboost (Notebook); Heathergreen. **87 123RF.com:** picsfive (clb). **Alamy Stock Photo:** David Cobb (crb). **Dreamstime.com:** Nomadsoul1 (bc). **Courtesy of National Park Service, Lewis and Clark National Historic Trail:** NPS Photo (tr). **88–89 Dreamstime.com:** Daboost (Notebook); Dmytro Synelnychenko. **88 123RF.com:** baiterekmedia (cr). **Dreamstime.com:** Robynmac / Robyn Mackenzie (cl). **Getty Images:** Moment Open / Laura Olivas (b). **89 123RF.com:** picsfive (br). **Alamy Stock Photo:** Steve Shuey (tr). **Dorling Kindersley:** Tom Grey (cla). **Dreamstime.com:** Kellie Eldridge (crb); Nicholas Motto (fcrb). **90 Dreamstime.com:** Michael Rubin (cb). **Shutterstock.com:** Worldswildlifewonders (bl). **90–91 Dreamstime.com:** Chernetskaya (Background); Daboost (Notebook). **91 123RF.com:** picsfive (clb); stillfx (tr). **Alamy Stock Photo:** Kevin Ebi (cb); Mark Miller Photos (r). **Dreamstime.com:** S Gibson (tl). **92–93 Dreamstime.com:** Daboost (Notebook); Selvam Raghupathy (Background). **92 123RF.com:** picsfive (tr). **Dreamstime.com:** Antonel (l); Irina Kozhemyakina (cra). **93 123RF.com:** sellphoto1 (cr); stillfx (crb). **Alamy Stock Photo:** Danita Delimont (bl). **Dreamstime.com:** Steve Byland (clb). **94 123RF.com:** stillfx (bl). **Alamy Stock Photo:** imageBROKER (cb). **Dreamstime.com:** Foster Eubank (tr). **94–95 Dreamstime.com:** Daboost (Notebook); Viacheslav Voloshyn (Background). **95 123RF.com:** picsfive (tl). **Alamy Stock Photo:** Robert E. Barber (bc). **iStockphoto.com:** Elizabeth M. Ruggiero (tr). **96 Alamy Stock Photo:** Agefotostock / Bret Edge (tr). **Dreamstime.com:** Golasza (c). **96–97 Dreamstime.com:** Daboost. **97 123RF.com:** picsfive (tr, crb). **Dreamstime.com:** Rinus Baak (bc); Melani Wright (ca). **98 123RF.com:** picsfive (clb). **Alamy Stock Photo:** agefotostock / George Ostertag (cra); All Canada Photos / Bob Gurr (crb). **98–99 Dreamstime.com:** Daboost (Notebook); Tirachard Kumtanom. **99 123RF.com:** picsfive (br). **Dreamstime.com:** Torsten Kuenzlen (bc); Stan Shillingburg (cr). **iStockphoto.com:** thepicthing (tr). **100 123RF.com:** picsfive (cl). **Dreamstime.com:** Larry Metayer (c). **SuperStock:** Michael Durham / Minden Pictures (br). **100–101 Dreamstime.com:** Daboost (Notebook); Wangkun Jia (t); Radekgibran (Background). **101 123RF.com:** picsfive (tr). **Getty Images:** Matt Meadows (cr); Gary Berdeaux / MCT / Tribune News Service (bl). **102–103 Dreamstime.com:** Daboost (Notebook). **102 Alamy Stock Photo:** Steve Greenwood (c); John Elk III (br). **Dreamstime.com:** Robynmac / Robyn Mackenzie (tr). **103 123RF.com:** picsfive (cl). **Dreamstime.com:** Cheri Alguire (tc); Brian Lasenby (br); Jon Bilous (cra); Mihai Andritoiu (b); Jeffrey Holcombe (ca). **iStockphoto.com:** JustineG (crb). **104–105 Alamy Stock Photo:** Wild Places Photography / Chris Howes (cl). **Dreamstime.com:** Daboost (Notebook); Selvam Raghupathy. **104 123RF.com:** picsfive (br). **naturepl.com:** Michael Durham (tr). **105 123RF.com:** picsfive (crb). **Alamy Stock Photo:** Nature Picture Library / Paul D Stewart (tr). **Dreamstime.com:** Mikelane45 (tl). **106–107 Dreamstime.com:** Martin Schneiter. **108 Dreamstime.com:** Jaahnlieb (bc); Kcmatt (cra). **iStockphoto.com:** Frank Anschuetz (cb). **108–109 Dreamstime.com:** Daboost (Notebook); Ilmito. **109 123RF.com:** picsfive (tl, cr). **Dreamstime.com:** Humorousking207 (cl). **110 123RF.com:** stillfx (tl). **Alamy Stock Photo:** Clint Farlinger (bl). **Dreamstime.com:** Jason P Ross (t). **110–111 Dreamstime.com:** Daboost (Notebook); Harutyun Poghosyan (Background). **111 123RF.com:** stillfx (c). **Alamy Stock Photo:** Douglas Peebles Photography (tl); WaterFrame (bl). **Dreamstime.com:** The World Traveller (cr). **112–113 Alamy Stock Photo:** Pat & Chuck Blackley (c). **Dreamstime.com:** Daboost (Notebook); Natalia Shabasheva (Background). **112 Alamy Stock Photo:** Danita Delimont (bl). **Dreamstime.com:** Robert Roach (cra). **113 123RF.com:** picsfive (tl). **Alamy Stock Photo:** Nature Picture Library (bl). **Dreamstime.com:** Kenneth Keifer (tr); Robynmac / Robyn Mackenzie (br). **114 123RF.com:** stillfx (br). **Alamy Stock Photo:** Ken Barber (cra). **Dorling Kindersley:** Liberty's Owl, Raptor and Reptile Centre, Hampshire, UK. (bl). **114–115 Dreamstime.com:** Daboost (Notebook). **115 123RF.com:** picsfive (cl). **Alamy Stock Photo:** Spring Images (cr); Stockimo / dimple (tr). **Dreamstime.com:** Alan Dyck (bc). **116 123RF.com:** picsfive (cra). **Alamy Stock Photo:** National Geographic Image Collection (crb). **Dreamstime.com:** Stepanjezek (cl). **SuperStock:** Brian W. Downs / Aurora RF (bl). **116–117 Dreamstime.com:** Daboost (Notebook); Dmytro Synelnychenko (Background). **117 123RF.com:** stillfx (cl). **Alamy Stock Photo:** Patrick Kennedy (cra); Jim West (ca). **Library of Congress, Washington, D.C.:** LC-DIG-highsm-40804 / Highsmith, Carol M., 1946 (bl). **118 123RF.com:** stillfx (cra). **Alamy Stock Photo:** George H.H. Huey (br). **Dreamstime.com:** Brian Lasenby (c); Alexander Shalamov (cl). **118–119 Dreamstime.com:** Daboost (Notebook). **119 123RF.com:** picsfive (cl). **Alamy Stock Photo:** Nature Picture Library (br); NPS Photo (cra). **120 123RF.com:** picsfive (cr). **Dreamstime.com:** Natalia Bachkova (ca); Zrfphoto (cl); Sandra Foyt (clb/Bathhouse); William Wise (br); Yellowdesignstudio (clb). **120–121 Dreamstime.com:** Daboost (Notebook); Christian De Grandmaison (Background). **121 123RF.com:** stillfx (crb). **Alamy Stock Photo:** Ian Dagnall (tr). **Dreamstime.com:** F11photo (b); Joanne Stemberger (cla). **122 123RF.com:** picsfive (ca, cl, cb, clb); stillfx (crb); Janek Sergejev (bc). **Dreamstime.com:** Natalia Bachkova (br); Bolotov (cra, cr). **123 123RF.com:** picsfive (cb). **Alamy Stock Photo:** Shawn Boss (bc). **Dreamstime.com:** Brandon Alms (br)

Endpaper images: *Front:* **123RF.com:** Marina Scurupii; *Back:* **123RF.com:** Marina Scurupii

Cover images: *Front:* **Dreamstime.com:** Minyun Zhou / Minyun9260 cra, Stockoxinoxi t, Stockoxinoxi br; **Getty Images:** WIN-Initiative; *Back:* **Alamy Stock Photo:** Radek Hofman bl; **iStockphoto.com:** sorincolac tl